NEW YORK'S 50 BEST

—

Places
to Discover
and Enjoy in
Central Park

KAREN PUTNAM & MARIANNE CRAMER

Central Park
Conservancy

FOREWORD BY TOM BROKAW
DRAWINGS BY JOHN COBURN

CITY & COMPANY · NEW YORK

Note to Readers:
Please turn to pages 138 and 139
for a map of the Park.

Copyright © 1999 by Karen Putnam & Marianne Cramer
Central Park Conservancy
All rights reserved. No portion of this book may be reproduced
without permission of the publisher.

New York's 50 Best Cover Concept
Copyright © 1995 by Nancy Steiny
Cover and Text of *Places to Discover and Enjoy in Central Park*
Copyright © 1999 by Heather Zschock
Drawings copyright © 1999 by John Coburn

Library of Congress Cataloging-in-Publication Data
Putnam, Karen. New York's 50 best places to discover and enjoy
in central park/Karen Putnam & Marianne Cramer.
p.cm.
Includes Index.
ISBN 1-885492-64-2
I. Central Park (New York, N.Y.) Guidebooks. 2. New York
(N.Y.) Guidebooks. I. Cramer, Marianne. II. Title. III. Title:
New York's fifty best places to discover and enjoy in Central Park.
F128.65.C3P87 1999
917.47'1—dc21
99-20604
CIP
Printed in the United States of America
First Edition

To my son Lowell Putnam,
who helps keep my eye on
what matters in life.

In Memoriam
To my father Roy Cramer,
for teaching me the secret
language of the land.

ACKNOWLEDGEMENTS

There may be a creative formula that dictates the slimmer the volume, the more extensive the acknowledgments; it certainly applies in this case. The Central Park Conservancy is blessed with people of passion and expertise; they are behind all the "stories" in the book. *Neil Calvanese* has confirmed our horticultural references. *Sara Cedar Miller* has checked for historical veracity. *Jennifer Wald* has supplied her fine public relations hand. Thanks to *Doug Blonsky* and *Eve Rothenberg*, too, for checking the checkers. Of course, there would have been scant need for the book without the Park's restoration. For that extraordinary accomplishment New York has many far-sighted individuals to thank, but particularly we thank *Elizabeth Barlow Rogers*, the Conservancy's founder, and *Gordon Davis*, the Parks Commissioner under Mayor Edward Koch, who championed the Conservancy's cause in 1980. In 1998 Conservancy Chairman *Ira M. Millstein*, *Mayor Rudolph Giuliani*, and Parks Commissioner *Henry J. Stern* initiated a bold and innovative phase in the public/private partnership between the City and the Conservancy; they signed a contract assigning to the Conservancy management responsibility for Central Park. We salute their vision in partnering to preserve the good work of the last two decades.

The Conservancy and City together must thank the many donors whose gifts have made possible Central Park's renaissance. And we salute the extraordinary work of the Conservancy's *Women's Committee*, a volunteer group without peer that raises funds and friends on behalf of our Park.

Two publications were especially valuable resources in our research: *The Art Commission and the Municipal Art Society Guide to Manhattan's Outdoor Sculpture* by Margot Gayle and Michele Cohen and *The Park and the People: A History of Central Park* by Roy Rosenzweig and Elizabeth Blackmar. We referred often to these works and recommend them to others interested in our great Park.

Our acknowledgments would not be complete without recognizing the work of our talented editor, *Theresa Burns*, the charming artwork of *John Coburn*, and finally the patient, painstaking persistence, and irreplaceable hard work of the Conservancy's *Drena Peterson* in preparing entry after entry, version after version. This book simply would not be here—certainly not in our lifetimes—without Drena.

Thank you, to you all.

Contents

FOREWORD

Central Park is one of the urban wonders of the world, a green heart in the great concrete, high-rise landscape of New York City. It is so naturally a part of the Manhattan environment many people may not realize it is entirely man-made.

But what every Park visitor does know is that Central Park is a haven. It is a place where all of us can alter the frenetic rhythms that make New York the most exciting City in the world. We can sit on a bench and read the paper, toss a ball with friends, jog, cycle, or play with our children. Connections with Central Park run especially deep with New Yorkers. We tend to think of the Park as our own front yard. In true New York fashion, the Park reflects the stories of our diversified population.

It is hard to imagine that Frederick Law Olmsted and Calvert Vaux, the designers of Central Park, could have foreseen the impact the Park has had on the lives of so many people. They certainly knew their 1858 "Greensward Plan," the design for Central Park, was in the American grain: a master plan for the first major park intended entirely for public use. And they knew the Park would be a healthy refuge from the overcrowded living conditions in southern Manhattan. (After all, the City had been developed only to 38th Street when construction on Central Park began at 59th Street.) As true 19th-century romantics, they also trusted in the power of nature to lift man's spirits above the drudgery of City life. But could they have envisioned the skyscrapers and high-rise apartment buildings that provide the backdrop to so many Park views? Could they have anticipated over a quarter of a million people streaming into Central Park on a spring weekend?

Over the last few decades our "front yard" took heavy wear and tear—not surprising with about 20 million visitors a year. Landscapes had eroded, buildings were in disrepair, and graffiti covered almost every surface. Then in 1980, a not-for-profit group, the Central Park Conservancy, teamed up with the City to pool resources and talent to rescue and maintain the Park. Almost twenty years later, that innovative public/private partnership between the City and the Conservancy was contractually formalized and the Park has never looked better.

So what better time to explore (at least some of) the Park's 843 acres? This book offers new information about favorite destinations and will introduce you to a few places that you've probably never visited. You'll find some history, some anecdotes, and some horticulture—and some inspiration to get to know New York City's Central Park, the greatest public park in the world. Along the way be sure to acknowledge the genius of Frederick Law Olmsted and Calvert Vaux as well as the vision of far-sighted 19th-century City planners who anticipated the need for a park whose scale and democratic purpose had no precedent.

—Tom Brokaw

INTRODUCTION

When we first set out to write this book, we knew it would be a daunting task. Central Park means so much to so many people and each Park visitor has his or her own favorite place and special Park memory.

Central Park's 843 acres of rolling lawns, woodlands, and waterbodies can be overwhelming and mysterious to even the most native of New Yorkers. This book is designed to invite the exploration of all of Central Park by highlighting some of its more popular destinations. The 50 Best Places that we have selected here represent a combination of some of the best-known sites, like Sheep Meadow and Bethesda Fountain, as well as some of the lesser known locales, like the Ravine and the Park's military fortifications. We hope that you will visit each of these places first hand to see for yourself the variety of experiences Central Park has to offer.

We've tried to include a range of information in each entry, from horticultural details to historical facts and anecdotes to architectural distinctions. Most of all, we've tried to provide you an entertaining and informative book that will whet your curiosity and encourage many visits to Central Park.

Marianne Cramer, my co-author, who is a landscape architect and worked as the Central Park planner for fifteen years, notes the natural beauty of each place that we visit. I hold a doctorate in American Studies and take a keen interest in the cultural aspects of each locale.

If you are a New Yorker, or you visited Central Park in the 1970s, you will know that there has been a renaissance in the Park. Dusty, dying landscapes like the Great Lawn are now lush green carpets. Trash-filled waterbodies now have inviting shorelines and thriving ecosystems. This most recent rebirth of Central Park is due to New York City's partnership with the Central Park Conservancy, the private, not-for-profit organization formed in 1980 that manages Central Park under a contract with the City of New York Parks & Recreation. Through private donations from individuals, foundations, and corporations, the Conservancy provides more than 80 percent of the Park's annual operating budget, funds major capital improvements, provides horticultural care and management, and offers programs for volunteers and visitors. A portion of all proceeds from sales of this book will support the Conservancy in its effort to keep Central Park beautiful for all.

We hope that this book will inspire you to become a partner with the Conservancy and the City in taking care of the Park to ensure that it remains a beautiful place for leisure, recreation, and the appreciation of nature.

Karen H. Putnam
President
Central Park Conservancy

An Invitation to Tea

ALICE IN WONDERLAND

(official name: *Margarita Delacorte Memorial*)
East 74th Street, north of Conservatory Water
José de Creeft, sculptor

At the northern end of the model boat pond sits Central Park's most beloved sculpture, a bronze grouping of our favorite characters from Lewis Carroll's 1865 fantasy-laced classic *Alice's Adventures in Wonderland.* Alice herself holds court perched on a giant mushroom, reaching toward a pocket watch held by the March Hare, the host of the book's zany tea party. Her serenity contrasts sharply with the manic expression of the nearby Mad Hatter, who appears poised to launch into one of his non-sensical riddles. Crowding the edge of a smaller mushroom and nibbling on a tea goodie is the timid dormouse, who seems ready to flee any impending insult. And peering over Alice's shoulder in all the activity is the Cheshire Cat, Wonderland's very own gossip maven.

Philanthropist George Delacorte commissioned this sculpture from José de Creeft, in honor of Delacorte's wife, Margarita. Dedicated in 1959, de Creeft's sculpture closely follows Sir John Tenniel's whimsical Victorian illustrations from the first edition of the book. Alice her-self is said to resemble de Creeft's daughter, Donna. In the longstanding tradition of honoring a patron within a work of art, the sculptor may have included Delacorte himself by way of caricature as the Mad Hatter; it is probably best not to probe any symbolism there. The sculptor also included lines from Margarita's favorite poem, "The Jabberwocky," in a granite circle surrounding his work:

> *"Twas brillig, and the slithy toves*
> *did gyre and gimble in the wabe . . ."*

Successful in its own right as an engaging work of art, the sculpture attracts children who climb its many levels and explore the soothing textures of its surfaces. The bronze's glowing patina, polished by thousands of tiny hands, testifies to the popularity of this Central Park landmark.

A Twenty-one Gun Salute
THE ARSENAL

64th Street at Fifth Avenue
Open Monday—Friday 9 am—5 pm
Martin E. Thompson, architect
Constructed 1847—1853

The Arsenal has two claims to historical prominence. It is one of only two buildings within the Park walls that predate the Park (the other being the Block House built in the Northern Park for the War of 1812). Today the Arsenal houses the offices of the Parks Department City of New York and the Central Park Wildlife Conservation Center.

And, secondly, it is the current home of the "Greensward Plan," the original blueprint for Central Park created and drafted by Frederick Law Olmsted and Calvert Vaux. Olmsted and Vaux borrowed the name "Greensward" from the landscape term describing pastoral, open stretches of land; its 19th-century usage also implied the pastoral landscape's ability to introduce viewers to the notion of true beauty in nature.

The Arsenal was built in 1851 as a munitions supply depot for New York State's National Guard. The Guard chose the site because at that time it afforded an overview of the City to the south and could offer swift troop transport via the New York and Harlem Railroad. It is a picturesque, landmark, brick building designed to look like a medieval castle, complete with eight battlements. More decorative flourishes were added in 1935 with painted white "muskets" to support the stairway railing and cast iron replicas of military drums on either side of the door. WPA artist Allan Saalburg painted murals for the two-story lobby, depicting a montage of park scenes and troops in military formation. A rather incongruous multitiered crystal chandelier made by artisans from Czechoslovakia, a glamorous decorative fixture more appropriate for a ballroom than a military facility, hangs in the lobby.

The treasure of the Arsenal is not, however, the building itself, but the original rendering by Olmsted and Vaux of the Greensward Plan. Under glass in a large, third-floor conference room, the Greensward Plan is testimony to the vast scale of the Park and to the vision that went into creating one of the country's most important public spaces.

Our Best Friend as Hero

BALTO

East Drive at 66th Street
Frederick George Richard Roth, sculptor
Dedicated in 1925

An unexpected hero stands on a rock outcropping on the main path leading north from the Tisch Children's Zoo. A slightly larger-than-life bronze sculpture honors Balto, the Siberian husky who led a dogsled team through an Alaskan blizzard to deliver an antitoxin needed to halt a diphtheria epidemic. The driver of the team

described the trip to reporters at the time: "I couldn't see the trail. Many times I couldn't even see my dogs, so blinding was the gale. I gave Balto, my lead dog, his lead and trusted to him. He never once faltered. It was Balto who led the way. The credit is his." Sadly, Balto prevailed only to die as a result of the rigors of the journey. But recently his memory was recalled in an animated film that introduced Balto to a new generation of children.

In their book on Manhattan's outdoor sculpture (see bibliography), Margot Gayle and Michele Cohen provide not only the above information but also a description of the sculpture's details. Frederick G. R. Roth was a noted animal sculptor. His *Balto* is panting with his legs braced; the dogsled harness is hanging from his back, as he appears to survey the distance. The lifesize sculpture is made even more lifelike by its realistically carved musculature and fur. A low-relief plaque shows the dogsled team braving the blizzard. As is true of the *Alice in Wonderland* sculpture (see page 14), the glowing bronze reflects the loving pats of countless children, and perhaps of adults, as they happen on Balto near Willowdale Arch.

Horticulturists should take note of the Osage orange tree directly behind *Balto*, and down the path to the south a large sweetgum tree recognized by its star-shaped leaves.

A Hawk's Eye View

BELVEDERE CASTLE

Mid-Park at 79th Street

Perched on Vista Rock, the highest natural elevation in the Park, is Belvedere Castle. Belvedere—Italian for "beautiful view," offers visitors just that. You can look down into the Delacorte Theater to the left, home to summertime Public Theater productions of Shakespeare and cutting edge interpretations of new and classic plays. Straight ahead is the newly restored, 55-acre Great Lawn, once one of the Park's original reservoirs; it now offers softball fields, basketball courts, and an abundance of sunbathers. And below, replete with a boulder-strewn shoreline, is Turtle Pond (see page 131).

What about the Castle itself? Belvedere was designed by Frederick Law Olmsted and Calvert Vaux as a Victorian "folly." In architectural terms, a folly was a spot of playfulness, a fantasy building—a miniature Greek or Roman temple or a pint-sized Gothic castle—that offered a dash of the unexpected in a carefully calculated pastoral landscape. The Castle originally was only a shell, with open window frames and doorways; it was really just an elaborate scenic overlook.

Today Belvedere Castle has true windows and doors and is home to the Henry Luce Nature Observatory run by the Central Park Conservancy. Inside are simple displays that show how naturalists observe the world to learn how it works and how they share their findings. There are telescopes and microscopes and skeletons and feathers—all designed to pique the curiosity of young visitors.

On the Castle's second floor, papier mâché reproductions of birds often seen in Central Park roost in the branches of a plywood tree. (Few people know that Central Park, located on the Atlantic flyway, is one of the country's richest birdwatching areas.) By pushing a button on a recording box, visitors can also listen to the particular songs belonging to the birds in the "tree." Budding naturalists can borrow backpacks that contain binoculars, reference material, maps, and notepaper and take off to explore either the Ramble (home to many species of birds) or to study aquatic life at the edge of Turtle Pond.

If you have lived in the City for any length of time you've probably heard the phrase, "The Temperature in Central Park is . . ." The information comes from meteorological instruments located at Belvedere. In fact, data has been collected at this site by the U.S. Weather Bureau since 1919. Look for the automated meteorological equipment on the top of the peaked tower roof and in the fenced-in compound to the south of the castle. If you want to find out whether your picnic will be rained out, stop at the second floor to get an up-to-the-minute weather report.

The Hand of Man in the
Heart of the Park

BETHESDA TERRACE

Mid-Park at 72nd Street

In their master plan for Central Park, the 1858 "Greensward Plan," Frederick Law Olmsted and Calvert Vaux proposed an architectural "heart of the Park" defined by a sweeping promenade that would culminate in a terrace overlooking the Lake. *The Park and the People* quotes Vaux saying to a newspaper reporter in 1865, however, that the architecture was always to be subordinate to the landscape: "Nature first, 2nd and 3rd—architecture after a while."

Yet Olmsted and Vaux also understood the practical nature of a public park. There had to be places for people to gather, to experience the human variety the City had to offer, as well as the inspiration of nature. And they succeeded splendidly with Bethesda Terrace and what we now call the Mall (formerly the Promenade). Park visitors stand on the Upper Terrace and look across the Lake at the rugged shoreline of the Ramble. They look down on the lawn Terrace and watch classes of new mothers doing aerobics, using strollers for counterpoises. Or they watch rowboats and even an occasional gondola pass across the Lake's foreground. The scene is framed now—as it was before the turn of the century—by two twenty-foot ornamental poles bearing gonfalons, colorful medieval-style banners. Leaving the Upper Terrace, visitors can sit on benches built into the lawn's terrace walls and watch the human parade at eye-level.

The decorative elements for Bethesda Terrace itself were designed by English-born architect Jacob Wrey Mould. Reasserting the primacy of nature, Mould chose representative wildlife and seasonal design motifs. The sandstone carvings of birds and plants are so carefully rendered you can identify each species. There are also carvings symbolic of day: a rising sun, a crowing cock. Night is represented by a lamp and book, a bat and owl, and a witch flying over a jack-o'-lantern.

On the Lower Terrace is one of the most photographed fountains in the world, *Angel of the Waters*. *Bethesda Fountain*, as it is often called, was the only sculpture commissioned as part of the original design of the Park. The artist, Emma Stebbins, was the first woman to receive a commission for a major public work in New York City; the fact that she was the sister of Col. Henry G. Stebbins, the president of the Central Park Board of Commissioners, does not detract from her accomplishment or talent. The sculpture, dedicated in 1873, is a neoclassical winged female figure who symbolically blesses the water of the fountain with one hand and carries a lily, the symbol of purity, in the other. The fountain is meant to celebrate the opening of the Croton Aqueduct, which brought fresh water to New Yorkers in 1842.

A Ribbon of Cast Iron

BOW BRIDGE

**West of Bethesda Terrace
Connecting Cherry Hill and the Ramble
Built in 1862**

Bow Bridge is one of the most handsomely designed cast iron bridges in the world. It spans 60 feet across the Lake, linking the cultivated and flowering landscape of Cherry Hill with the rustic and sprawling woods of the Ramble. Its proportions and sinuous length inspired one visitor to remark that the bridge looked "poured" over the Lake.

Calvert Vaux, Frederick Law Olmsted's partner, designed Bow Bridge in 1859, mindful of the flexible engineering properties of iron. Vaux and Olmsted gener-

ally preferred that bridges and arches in Central Park be crafted from natural materials—such as granite and brownstone with brick, or bluestone, or warm Novia Scotia sandstone. Using these natural materials, they argued, would soften the intrusion of a man-made structure into the Park's "natural" setting. But in the case of Bow Bridge, cast iron was a clear ally in their design efforts; it allowed them to build a bridge that served as the perfect transition between the emphatically architectural statement of Bethesda Terrace and the abundant randomness of the Ramble.

City commissioners overseeing the building of Central Park also welcomed Bow Bridge, but they had a simpler reason: cost. Historians Rosenzweig and Blackmar note that by 1859 the commissioners projected that it would cost at least $3.6 million to build the Park—twice the authorized budget! While Olmsted and Vaux debated the aesthetic qualities of building materials, some commissioners eyed only the bottom line. The most cost-effective material for building bridges at that time was cast iron, since it eliminated masons' and stonecutters' labor costs.

The true "value" of Bow Bridge, completed in 1862, does not lie in construction ledgers, however, but in its extraordinary visual effect. It has been the romantic setting for wedding proposals, classic film shoots, and the choice of many photographers who want to capture one of the signature design features of Central Park.

THE BRIDLE PATH

Reservoir Loop, 1.5 miles
North Meadow Loop, 1.1 miles
Southern Spur, 1.5 miles

It may seem surprising that Frederick Law Olmsted and Calvert Vaux originally proposed only a modest bridle trail to accommodate horseback riding in Central Park. Many visitors today consider spying the occasional horseback rider part of the Park's serendipitous charm and a welcome flashback to an earlier era. In the late 19th and early 20th centuries, moreover, there were literally hundreds of stables in Manhattan where horses could be boarded or rented.

But it was the very ubiquity of horses throughout the City that gave Olmsted and Vaux pause. In that pre-automobile age, they wondered, why invite another distraction of City life into the bucolic refuge of the Park? In *The Park and the People*, we read that two powerful members of the City commission overseeing the Park's construction disagreed with the designers' priorities. Financier August Belmont and banker Robert Dillon shared a fondness for horseback riding. In the minutes from committee reports at the time, Dillon spoke of riding's "manly" attributes and "invigorating" effects. Belmont's lifestyle testified to his esteem for riding; his lavish stables were equipped with gaslights and running water—amenities rare even in peoples' homes in New York at the time.

Dillon and Belmont won out. The original plan to have the Bridle Trail loop only around the Reservoir was changed; additional loops were added to the north and to the south. The Northern Loop branches off from the Reservoir Loop just north of 96th Street. Then the Trail passes between the pastoral East Meadow and the contiguous North Meadow with its Recreation Center and twelve ballfields. The Trail heads north and turns west into the Park at 104th Street. The Trail then crosses the northern portion of the wooded Ravine and the Loch, and swings south, paralleling the West Drive. It passes the Tennis Courts and then reconnects with the Reservoir Loop.

Whereas the Northern Loop still follows its original design, the Southern Loop today differs from the 1860s original. It has surrendered part of its length to the Zoo, Wollman Rink, and the Heckscher Ballfields. The Southern Loop begins, as it first did, on the West Side, just

north of the 86th Street transverse road. It heads south, passing the Arthur Ross Pinetum (see page 114) to its east and Summit Rock (see page 122) to its west. It skirts the Great Lawn and swings south alongside Shakespeare Garden (see page 116) and the Swedish Cottage (see page 124). The Southern Loop then runs close along Central Park West, within sight of the American Museum of Natural History and the New York Historical Society. It passes the Lake to the east, and then the elegiac Strawberry Fields. Continuing south, the Trail passes the Sheep Meadow, Tavern on the Green, and Heckscher Ballfields, to end somewhat abruptly near Central Park South and Seventh Avenue. By way of compensation to its riders, the southern spur offers six recently restored arches whose names alone summon lyrical associations: Winterdale, Eaglevale, Rifstone, Dalehead, Greyshot, Pinebank.

Of New York's hundreds of earlier stables, only one remains operational today: Claremont Stables, established in 1892 as a public livery stable and the oldest continuously operating stable in the United States. Claremont is located two blocks from the Park on West 89th Street. There you can rent a horse, ride across Central Park West and experience the Park from an entirely new perspective. If you wait until December you can don formal hunting gear for Claremont's Annual Christmas Ride Classic. After a two-and-one-half hour ride through the Park, the group heads for Tavern on the Green to drink from the traditional stirrup cup and feed the horses carrots from a silver platter. August Belmont surely would have approved.

The Classic Childhood Memory
THE CAROUSEL

Mid-Park at 64th Street
Open daily April—November 10 am—6 pm,
weather permitting
Open November—April 10 am—4:30 pm,
weather permitting
Information: 212-879-0244

C entral Park's first carousel was built in 1870 and, according to Park lore, was turned by a blind mule and a horse. Whether this story is apocryphal or true, there is no question that the Carousel quickly became one of the Park's most popular features.

Park commissioners early on had been resistant to commercial enterprises in the Park but eventually saw public value in "amusements"—or "intrusions," as their detractors called them. Historians Roy Rosenzweig and Elizabeth

Blackmar note the Carousel's growing franchise fees to the City also confirmed the value of amusements. Soon pony and goat carts, boat and carriage rides, a photography house to take souvenir pictures, and even wheelchair rides with attendants opened up for business, along with the Carousel.

Today's Friedsam Memorial Carousel is the fourth carousel to exist on that site. Animal lovers will be glad to learn that around the turn of the century a steam-powered carousel replaced the animal-powered original. In 1924, however, that carousel was destroyed by fire, as was

its successor in 1950.

After a long search the Parks Department discovered the present vintage carousel, abandoned in the old trolley terminal on Coney Island. Crafted by the Brooklyn firm of Stein and Goldstein in 1908, the Carousel is one of the largest in the United States, with 58 hand-carved, painted horses. Stein and Goldstein were among the foremost carvers of their day and the horses—nearly life-size in the outer ring—are caught rearing or mid-stride with almost fierce reality.

The Carousel today still holds its magic charm, with almost 250,000 riders a year. A ride costs $.90 for adults (who enjoy the scale of the horses and the brisk speed of the ride), $.50 for children and senior citizens. During warm weather the admissions line snakes around hot dog and popcorn vendors, recalling the atmosphere of a country fair. The generations mingle, and the calliope provides the traditional soundtrack.

Visitors will want to check out the wrought iron fence that surrounds the open Carousel sides; small, brightly-painted horses are depicted on a band around the fence.

A Loaf of Bread, A Jug of Mineral Water, and You

CEDAR HILL

East Side between 76th and 79th Streets

C edar Hill is a classic pastoral landscape, synonymous in many people's minds with the most traditional of Park activities: picnicking, reading, and (despite the thinning ozone) sunbathing. Cedar Hill undulates softly down to a shallow green valley. Its name comes from the red cedars on its crest, but several other varieties of evergreen dot the hill as well. At the southern border is Glade Arch, a handsome stone archway that originally supported carriage traffic to Fifth Avenue. In springtime, a variety of flowering

bulbs and perennials crowd the slopes on either side of the pathway under the arch. To the north is the Metropolitan Museum of Art.

Just as Olmsted and Vaux intended, the combination of lush grass, sun, and shade made Cedar Hill a landscape destination, a site that stood a world apart from the City's grid and traffic. But over time heavy use took its toll. A 1994 restoration included new irrigation, repaired and improved drainage (clay drainage pipes dating from the 1860s still snake underground throughout the Park), and replanted grass. But most importantly, at that time the Central Park Conservancy introduced a new management system, dividing the Park into 49 zones, each with its own gardener and support team.

In the spirit of "nothing new under the sun," one aspect of the maintenance technique was first piloted in the 1880s at Sheep Meadow. According to those early posted instructions, when "the turf of the green Sheep Meadow is not specifically unfit for use," a variety of activities were allowed on a rotating basis: ballplaying on Saturdays; croquet playing on Mondays, Wednesdays, and Fridays; the public in general on Sunday. A color-coded flag system signaled proper usage. Today's system uses only one color: red. At Cedar Hill today (and at the Great Lawn) red flags alert the public to horticultural care being performed or adverse lawn conditions (such as wetness after a rain, when grass is vulnerable to damage), requiring the landscape to "take a breather" from use. When the red flag comes down, it's back to books, hampers, and lotion.

Polar and Temperate and Tropical, Oh My!

CENTRAL PARK WILDLIFE CENTER AND TISCH CHILDREN'S ZOO

East Side between 63rd and 66th Streets
Open Monday—Friday 10 am—5 pm
Admission: adults $3.50; children 3—12 $.50
Information: 212-861-6030 • Café and Gift Shop

Although most New Yorkers still call it the Zoo, the Central Park Wildlife Center is eager to shed the old name. They believe "zoo" connotes small cages for animals and concrete floors for "habitat" with no commitment to the conservation of threatened and endangered species. Central Park's state-of-the-art Wildlife Center was built after the Wildlife Conservation Society took over as managers in 1984. It showcases animals from tropical, temperate, and polar zones around the world.

A favorite with many visitors is the sea lion pool in the center courtyard. Probably the most popular exhibit at the old Central Park Zoo, a new design features glass sides so visitors can see these sleek carnivorous mammals gliding and spiraling under water. During feeding time (11:30 am, 2 pm, and 4 pm) the quartet of seals performs simple tricks for their meal. Equally fine is the lush perennial garden surrounding the pool, with benches tucked into corners. Of course, the nearby backstroking polar bear is a year-round attraction, lolling center stage in his watery miniwilderness.

Visitors can see vestiges of the old zoo preserved in the new. Limestone reliefs by Frederick George Richard Roth of antelopes, birds, monkeys, lions, and wolves from the old animal houses have been incorporated into the new buildings.

The newest addition to the Wildlife Center is the Tisch Children's Zoo. Probably the most popular with the stroller set are the domestic animal areas around the perimeter. Here children can get close to goats, sheep, a cow, and a Vietnamese pot-bellied pig. A quarter in one of the dispensers will buy a handful of nutritious food for the animals to nibble out of your hand. Small bronze sculptures of the animals stand next to each pen. When a

child touches a sculpture it emits the appropriate cry or squawk. Also in the area are models of giant turtle shells, fish heads, and rabbit ears that demonstrate the mechanisms of sight, sound, and body structure.

In the center of the Children's Zoo is the Enchanted Forest. Artisans mimicked the colossal remains of primeval oak trees, acorns, and a giant spider. In the central aviary—actually a complete habitat—you will see live turtles and frogs along with birds. One of the two children's theaters is in the central aviary. The other theater is in the central courtyard. A troupe of actors at the Acorn Theater in the Tisch Children's Zoo perform daily shows for children about animals. Past shows include *I Eat Bugs* and *Metamorphosis Boogie*.

Between the Wildlife Center and the Children's Zoo is the George Delacorte Musical Clock built on a triple archway of brick. Every hour on the hour one of 32 nursery-rhyme tunes play while a bear with a tambourine, a hippopotamus with a violin, a goat with pan pipes, a kangaroo and offspring with horns, and a penguin with a drum glide around the base of the clock. At the top of the clock two monkeys appear to strike a bell. On the half-hour, the mechanical performance is a bit shorter, but still delightful. The audience for the clock's performance is a tableau of anticipation: parents pointing out each animal's ballet move to their children, and the children's faces flushed with wonder at what will happen next. On the north side of the arches is Frederick George Richard Roth's *Honey Bear* sculpture dating from 1935.

Victorian Whimsy Amidst
Natural Beauty

CHERRY HILL AND WAGNER'S COVE

**West of Bethesda Terrace
Mid-Park at 72nd Street**

C herry Hill offers a Bethesda Terrace experience in miniature. From the rise of Cherry Hill, you also can see across the Lake to the abundant landscape of the Ramble.

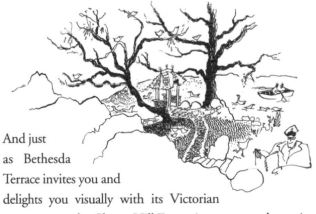

And just as Bethesda Terrace invites you and delights you visually with its Victorian ornament, so the Cherry Hill Fountain serves as a decorative arts destination in its own whimsical right.

Jacob Wrey Mould, Calvert Vaux's assistant, designed the decorative elements for Bethesda Terrace in 1859 and is also responsible for the fountain at Cherry Hill. He clearly pulled out all the stops for this 1860s creation. The ornamental finial on the fountain's top, the gilded cups brimming over with water, the frosted glass globes for lighting, a sculpted bluestone basin inset with Minton tiles—all for a watering trough for horses. Cherry Hill was intended to be a scenic turn-around for carriages, a place to admire the surrounding cherry trees' blooms in springtime and to take in the lakeside view.

Today Cherry Hill is a restful destination for sun-bathing or reading. A short walk west down a nearby slope leads to Wagner Cove, one of Central Park's hidden oases of calm. Tucked away into a shady corner of the Lake, the Cove features a small rustic wood shelter. The original shelters date from the Park's first years, when rowboats would crisscross the Lake, picking up passengers at one of several shelters that dotted the edge of the Lake and dropping them off at another. Today there is no row-boat ferry service, but the charm of the site remains.

The Gardens of Europe
in Manhattan

CONSERVATORY
GARDEN

East Side between 104th and 106th Streets
Open 8 am to dusk
Quiet zone

Reminiscent of a setting from a Merchant/Ivory film, Conservatory Garden is Central Park's only *formal* garden. It takes its name from the huge glass conservatory that once stood on this same spot, built in 1898. In 1934, when maintenance of the facility had become too costly, the Conservatory was demolished and replaced with the present Garden, which opened to the public in 1937. Conservatory Garden is in fact *three* gardens representing different landscape styles: Italian, French, and English.

To enter the six-acre Garden from Fifth Avenue, you must pass through the Vanderbilt Gates, which originally stood before the Vanderbilt Mansion at Fifth Avenue and 58th Street, the site of today's Bergdorf Goodman store. An Italian-style garden opens immediately before you. It is a restful oasis of formal green lawns and clipped hedges, bordered to the north and south by alleés of crabapple trees, and to the west by a wrought iron wisteria pergola. An elegant geyser fountain in front of the pergola provides a vertical contrast to the rows of hedges.

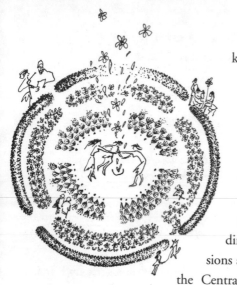

Few New Yorkers know that on the walkway under the pergola are medallions inscribed with the names of the original thirteen states. The Italian garden is the site of many wedding photography sessions and, in the spring, of the Central Park Conservancy Women's Committee's Frederick Law Olmsted Luncheon—dubbed the "American Ascot" for the abundance of hats!

To the north is the classical French-style garden. At its center is German sculptor Walter Schott's *Three Dancing Maidens*, which dates from approximately 1910. (It is also called *The Untermeyer Fountain*, after the family who presented it to the City in 1947.) Three smiling young women in bronze link hands as they dance around the fountain's spray; water also bubbles from grinning masks on the sides of the fountain's limestone base. Each young woman depicted is distinct, but their gestures and hairstyles and swirling dresses combine to express a love of life. Surrounding the fountain are concentric parterres (beds of plants arranged to create a design). And around the parterres are beds planted for two dazzling floral displays. In the spring, 20,000 tulips bloom; bulbs are planted anew each fall and the prior year's bulbs are given to neighborhood gardening groups. In the fall, 2,000 Korean chrysanthemums bloom in an ever-changing, but always brilliant, palette.

The southern garden is English in style. Sheltered in the center is a bronze sculpture of two children, Mary and Dicken, characters in Frances Hodgson Burnett's book *The Secret Garden.* The statue was created by Bessie Potter Vonnoh and installed in 1936. The children are on a pedestal—Dicken playing a flute and Mary listening—in the center of a reflecting pool where water lilies float in the summer. Perennials surround the sculpture with a variety of colors and textures throughout the year. The newest horticultural addition to the southern garden is a woodland slope along its outer perimeter—a shade garden using native plants combined with European and American species, the woodland slope is particularly lovely in the spring.

A Model of Boat Races

CONSERVATORY WATER

East Side between 72nd and 75th Streets
Kerbs Boathouse Ice Cream Café and
Central Park Sailboat Concession

Conservatory Water, Central Park's famous model boat pond, owes its existence to 19th-century City budget cuts in the building of Central Park. A model of how financial constraints can inspire creative alternatives, Conservatory Water was Frederick Law Olmsted and Calvert Vaux's response to Park Commissioners' demands that they abandon their original plans to build a massive conservatory on that site. The designers then looked to Paris for inspiration, where it was common to see children with rubber-tipped poles propelling tiny yachts on model-boat ponds. Much larger than its Paris counterparts, however, Conservatory Water invited American-style modifications. Soon radio-powered sailboats skippered by adults joined the child-prodded versions. Today visitors can watch a radio-powered racing regatta between members of the Model Yacht Club (a wing of the Kerbs Boathouse food concession), or cheer on children with their tiny wind-powered sloops, or even rent a miniature boat from a nearby concessionaire's wagon. (Visitors familiar with E. B. White's eponymous *Stuart Little* will remember the dapper mouse piloting his own yacht in a Conservatory Water regatta.)

The landscape surrounding Conservatory Water is notable in its own right. Hundreds of visitors enjoy sledding down Pilgrim Hill (named for John Quincy Adams Ward's 1885 bronze sculpture on its crest) as well as ice skating on the Pond, when nature cooperates. Horticulturists will spot a pawpaw and two crepe myrtle trees here, as well as seven species of oak. At the southern end of Conservatory Water are springtime billows of Yoshino cherries. Birders flock to that area to watch for red-tailed hawks, who have set up housekeeping on a Fifth Avenue apartment ledge.

Adding to the appeal of this site for children is the fabulous *Alice in Wonderland* sculpture to the north of the pond (see page 14) and the Hans Christian Andersen sculpture (by Georg John Lober, dedicated in 1956) to its west. Andersen sits on a bench with a book spread open on his legs—his lanky frame inviting children to climb up and listen to the story. A two-foot-high duck pauses attentively at his feet, presumably waiting to hear the happy ending of "The Ugly Duckling" tale.

Your Moo-ve

THE DAIRY AND CHESS AND CHECKERS HOUSE

East Side at 65th Street
Visitor Information Center and
Recreation Building
Open Tuesday—Sunday 10 am—5 pm
Closes at 4 pm in winter

At the end of a long ride north to the new Central Park, 19th-century children could enjoy a fresh, wholesome glass of milk at the Dairy. In the 1850s, residential Manhattan reached only as far north as 38th Street. During that time, New York City suffered from milk scandals. Some tainted milk, from cows in the southern parts of the City that were fed brewery mash instead of hay, was being sold commercially throughout the City. Fresh milk was worth seeking out. In addition, diphtheria outbreaks in the densely populated areas sent anxious families in search of healthier environments for their children. Although the Dairy design postdated the 1858 Greensward Plan, Olmsted and Vaux had always thought of the southernmost part of the Park as the Children's District, since it was the first arrival point for traveling families.

The Dairy design is a vintage Victorian hybrid: Swiss chalet meets Gothic country church. One half of the Dairy is an open loggia, made of wood with geometric gingerbread borders. The other half is a granite structure with window treatments and spires reminiscent of a country church. Olmsted and Vaux designed the loggia to catch both cool summer breezes from the Pond and as much warmth as the winter sun could offer. The view from the loggia south is framed by two tree-crowned bedrock outcrops. Historically, the focus of the view was the shoreline of the Pond; today it is colorful Wollman Rink, with the midtown skyline as backdrop.

The Dairy today serves as a general visitors center with a permanent exhibit on the history and design of the Park. There is a segmented flip map that shows how Olmsted and Vaux built Central Park from central Manhattan's original land forms, as well as photographs that show before-and-after examples of the extensive restoration of the Park begun by the Central Park Conservancy and the City in 1980.

To the west of the Dairy, on a large bedrock outcrop (called the Kinderberg or "children's mountain") stands the brick Chess and Checkers House. The City built the house in 1952 to replace the Park's largest and most ornate rustic wood summer house. Players from around the City gather at the 24 chess tables under a modern-day pergola to match wits and enjoy the summer shade.

CHARLES A. DANA DISCOVERY CENTER

Mid-Park at 110th Street
Family and Community Programs and Visitors Center
Open Tuesday—Sunday 10 am—5 pm
Closes at 4 pm in winter

Perched on the northern shore of the Harlem Meer, the Park's northernmost body of water, is Central Park's newest building. The Charles A. Dana Discovery Center so effectively follows Calvert Vaux's eclectic architectural style that you have to look very closely to note its modern-day origin. First opened to the public in 1993, it serves as the Upper Park's visitors' center and home to a wide variety of the Central Park Conservancy's free family and community programs.

The Park north of 96th Street is more rugged and picturesque than its southern counterpart. The pre-Park northern terrain was itself wilder, with large rocky outcroppings amidst low-lying areas. When Olmsted and Vaux first surveyed the proposed Park land, they decided that a rugged terrain would be the ideal complement to their southern pastoral vision. They also decided that it would be far too costly to significantly reshape the natural northern geography. In fact, pragmatism dictated the extension of the Park from its original northern border of

106th Street to 110th Street; it was simply too expensive for commercial developers to demolish and rebuild in that rocky and swampy area.

Today the City has grown up and far beyond the Park's northern borders, and enthusiasm for the area has grown as well. Many visitors consider the newly restored Harlem Meer one of the Park's most beautiful landscapes. Swans nest on Duck Island in the Meer and cormorants patrol the shoreline for fish. Birds are not the only ones eyeing the waters: fishing at the Harlem Meer has become a favorite family and community pastime. The Dana Discovery Center provides poles, unbarbed hooks (only catch and release is allowed), and instruction booklets. There is even a fishing jamboree celebrated each year after Labor Day.

The Dana Discovery Center offers seasonal exhibits in its Great Hall, often in collaboration with other cultural institutions in the City. Outside the Great Hall is a small deck overlooking the Meer with an unimpeded vista of the Park's landscape to the south. Educational programs are held throughout the year upstairs.

Adjacent to the Center is a small plaza where jazz concerts and other events (such as the Halloween Pumpkin Sail, when, at dusk, lit jack-o'-lanterns float across the Meer) take place. Young plantings of bald cypress, red maple, and weeping willows—all trees that thrive at the water's edge—surround the plaza.

All the Park's a Stage

DELACORTE THEATER

**Mid-Park at 80th Street
Southwest corner of the Great Lawn
Seasonal**

As New York impresario Joseph Papp figured out, if "the play's the thing" then the Park's the place. The Delacorte Theater is the summer home of the Public Theater/New York Shakespeare Festival. Papp began Shakespeare in the Park on a shoestring budget in 1957. Fueled by philanthropy and royalties from certain Broadway hits—notably *A Chorus Line*—the Public Theater has brought great open-air theater free to New Yorkers. All you need is the patience to wait in line for a ticket—a process that in itself has become a New York tradition. Tickets are distributed at 1 pm on the day of the performance. The line starts forming by 10 am, however; the veterans are identifiable by their books

and picnic hampers. The Public Theater recently started distributing tickets from 1–3 pm as well from their Astor Place home at 425 Lafayette Street.

The Shakespeare Marathon was Joseph Papp's plan to produce all of Shakespeare's plays at the Delacorte or the Public Theater. The Marathon began in 1987 with *Much Ado About Nothing*, and ended in 1997 with *Henry VIII*. The Delacorte also has hosted classical plays such as *Electra, Agamemnon*, and *The Skin of Our Teeth*, as well as musicals, including *The Pirates of Penzance* and *On the Town*. The list of well-known actors who have appeared at the Delacorte is a "Who's Who" of theater: George C. Scott, Kevin Kline, Blythe Danner, Denzel Washington, Richard Dreyfuss, Gregory Hines, Raul Julia, and Michelle Pfeiffer. And that's just a sampling.

Originally built as a temporary structure in 1962, the Delacorte Theater is still in place and is in the process of getting a facelift. The setting for the open-air theater is without peer. The audience sits in a horseshoe shape, just short of being in the round. The backdrop to the stage is Turtle Pond, bathed in the shifting shimmer of artificial lighting. Beyond the Pond is the velvety green of the Great Lawn. And to the right, perched on Vista Rock, is Belvedere Castle, profiled in a spotlight.

How Green Is Our Valley

THE DENE

East Side between 66th and 72nd Streets

The Dene (a term meaning "valley") is a long stretch of eastside landscape that exemplifies both the design features and the intended effect of Olmsted's pastoral vision. The Dene offers gently rolling lawns and shaded walks. For some Park visitors it is simply a route to another destination, such as Conservatory Water to the north or the zoo to the south. But the Dene should be relished for its own charm, as its own destination.

At its northern end is a verdant meadow called the East Green. At one point a boys' cricket field, it is once again the lawn Olmsted intended—a place for quiet reflection or reading or admiring the surrounding

Kwanzan cherry trees, crabapples, and magnolias in bloom. At the southern end is the summerhouse, a rustic wood shelter atop an imposing rock outcrop. (The Park today has three rustic wood structures like this one.) The Dene summerhouse is the perfect place to catch a breeze or take in the view. From the inside you can see the basic skeleton of its design, including the central post that supports the roof. The juxtaposition of this quaint structure against the Fifth Avenue skyline is another reminder that the Park was designed to be a refuge from the City.

Sophisticated Ladies and Gentleman

DUKE ELLINGTON CIRCLE

110th Street at Fifth Avenue
Dedicated July 1997

The sculpture of Edward Kennedy Ellington at 110th Street and Fifth Avenue is the first monument in New York City dedicated to an African American and the first memorial in the United States to Ellington. A composer, orchestra conductor, and musician, "Duke" Ellington elevated jazz to perhaps the most American of art forms. Blues-oriented players such as Johnny Hodges and Cootie Williams played with him, helping to shape

his style and inspire his compositions. The December 1927 opening at the Cotton Club—the showplace of Harlem speakeasies—put the Duke Ellington Orchestra on the jazz map. With Harlem and the Cotton Club as home base, Ellington began radio broadcasts and recorded for American, English, and French labels. Between 1930 and 1942 he was at his most creative, composing such classics as "Take the A Train" (later the Band's theme), "Mood Indigo," "Sophisticated Lady," "In a Sentimental Mood," and "Don't Get Around Much Anymore." Increasingly recognized as a major American composer, he received the Presidential Medal of Freedom in 1969.

On July 1, 1997, Robert Graham's *Duke Ellington Memorial* was unveiled at the northeast corner of Central Park. Politicians, dignitaries, and Harlem neighborhood residents mingled in the noonday sun to celebrate the culmination of an effort begun in 1979. Pianist Bobby Short conceived the project, headed fundraising efforts, and coordinated the selection of Robert Graham, a major sculptor of public art, to design the memorial. The result is a black patina bronze tableau 25-feet high, with an eight-foot-tall sculpture of Ellington standing next to an open grand piano. Supporting Ellington and the piano are three 10-foot-tall columns, each topped with three nude caryatid female figures representing the muses. The monument itself is situated within the Duke Ellington Circle, which is comprised of two, stepped, semicircular plazas that form an amphitheater.

The General and the Goddess

GRAND ARMY PLAZA

Fifth Avenue between 58th and 60th Streets
The Sherman Monument (dedicated 1903)
Pulitzer Fountain, Pomona (dedicated 1916)

Completed in 1916, Grand Army Plaza is considered one of the most successful urban plazas in the country. It is a focal point of midtown Manhattan offering an elegant transition to the Park from nearby skyscrapers such as the General Motors Building (softened in its ground-floor severity by the fanciful FAO Schwarz Toy Store clock near the building's southern entrance). The Grand Army Plaza is, in fact, two plazas—each a semicircle bisected by Central Park South. Both halves are surrounded on their curvilinear ends with Bradford Callery pear trees, which provide a natural frame. The split plaza was inspired by the design of the Place de la Concorde in Paris.

The Plaza takes its name from the Grand Army of the Potomac, the Union Army in the American Civil War. The northern half features a gilded bronze statue of Union General William Tecumseh Sherman, whose 1864 March to the Sea through the southern states cut the Confederacy in half, effectively ending the Civil War. The monument is by the famous sculptor Augustus Saint-Gaudens and ranks among the most distinguished equestrian groupings in western art. In 1888 Saint-Gaudens had modeled a bust of

Sherman from life and used that portrait for the equestrian statue, complete with Sherman's "creased and stubbled face and squared shoulders," as described by Margot Gale and Michele Cohen in their book on Manhattan's outdoor sculpture. Complementing that realistic portrait is the allegorical figure of victory, striding forward with upraised arm. This was Saint-Gaudens's last major work and fulfilled his desire to acknowledge the heroes of our Civil War.

The centerpiece in the southern half is quite different in concept and composition: the *Pulitzer Fountain* designed by Karl Bitter and dedicated in 1916. The fountain recalls Italian Renaissance fountains with its six granite basins rising upward, decreasing in size, and crowned with a graceful bronze figure of Pomona, goddess of abundance.

Giant rams-head horns of plenty flank both sides of the fountain. Pomona herself leans forward, her bare backside visible from the Vanderbilt mansion (formerly where Bergdorf Goodman now stands)—a placement by the sculptor some have said was intentional for more than design reasons.

To the north of Grand Army Plaza is the Doris C. Freedman Plaza, site of rotating six-month sculpture installations organized by the Public Art Fund. It is also prime brown-bag territory, as workers from surrounding buildings flock—with the pigeons—to benches around the Plaza and inside the Park. During their midday break, they can watch portrait artists or even the occasional organ grinder with his monkey.

THE GREAT HILL

West Side between 103rd and 107th Streets

The Great Hill is an open-hilltop meadow with picnic tables, a three-quarter mile soft-surface oval path (good for a jog), and green grass under stately American elms. The site has become known recently for "Great Jazz on the Great Hill," an annual summer music concert sponsored by the Central Park Conservancy that honors jazz musicians and their music. Late on a summer afternoon, 300 to 400 people gather to listen to legendary players like Billy Taylor, Max Roach, Gloria Lynne, or Roy Hargrove.

Although jazz seems a natural in this setting, Olmsted and Vaux originally had a much different use in mind for their landscape. They designed the Great Hill, the third highest elevation in the Park, as a carriage concourse where passengers could enjoy commanding views of the Hudson River and the Palisades. Just like Summit Rock (see page 122), the Great Hill was, however, more than an elevation with a view. It

was a stage where New Yorkers could display their affluence, distinguish themselves from other classes, and even establish a pecking order within their own class. *The New York Herald* in this regard called Central Park "the great rendezvous of the polite world."

But with the passing of time, and the growth of trees, the view slowly disappeared. For many years the Great Hill seemed to the majority of Park users a landscape in search of a purpose. Ideas for grand structures—Grant's tomb or a monument to the laying of the transatlantic cable—came and went. The restoration of the landscape in 1993 as a place for community leisure finally gave the Great Hill the contemporary identity it needed. It is now the site of family and church picnics, Frisbee games, running or racewalking on the oval track—all within the surrounding woods of magnificent American and English elms.

And then, one late afternoon each summer, jazz takes over. People stretch out on the lawn, prop their heads on their hands, shade their eyes from the setting sun, and let the music do the rest.

A Swinging Time

THE GREAT LAWN

Mid-Park between 79th and 86th Streets

Where else in Central Park can you have an alfresco dinner on a luxurious carpet of emerald-green grass and listen to a world-renowned symphony or opera? Only on the newly-restored Great Lawn. Every summer the New York Philharmonic and the Metropolitan Opera each give two free performances. On those nights a carpet of picnic blankets covers the lawn, and the Manhattan skyline defines the most famous Park view in the world. During the daytime a livelier tempo dominates, as Park users enjoy eight softball fields or play soccer, basketball, and volleyball.

Although integral to the lives of many New Yorkers and definitive in many ways of Central Park, the Great Lawn was not included in the Greensward Plan; it is the single largest landscape feature in the Park that was not part of Olmsted and Vaux's original design. One-hundred-dred-and-fifty years ago it was a 33-acre, rectangular receiving reservoir holding 180 million gallons of drinking water piped in from the Croton River in Westchester County. The reservoir predated Central Park and required Olmsted and Vaux to design their pastoral, naturalistic landscape around its hard-edged, rectangular shape.

The Croton Reservoir (completed in 1842) was adjacent to an older receiving reservoir, irregular in outline, which is now named the Jacqueline Kennedy Onassis Reservoir. A 1917 plan for a new water tunnel retained the original reservoir but rendered the Croton Reservoir obsolete. An extensive public debate over its use ensued, with suggestions ranging from sunken gardens to sports stadiums. Finally, in 1934, the City filled in the Croton Reservoir using, among other material, stones from the construction of Rockefeller Center. A 15-acre oval lawn took the Reservoir's place with a small pond at its southern end and two playgrounds at the northern end. In the 1950s eight ballfields were added. Within time the Great Lawn, as it was called, became the venue for some of the City's biggest outdoor events including the Paul Simon

concert, Disney's June 1995 preview of the movie *Pocahontas,* and a papal mass in October 1995 with Pope John Paul II.

Heavy use of this popular and central site took its toll. By the 1970s the Great Lawn was called the Great Dustbowl, with winds whipping up dry dirt from its compacted surface. A major renovation from 1996 to 1998 rescued the Great Lawn from New York's tough love. Working within the engineering constraints of the old Croton Reservoir, which had been filled but not removed, the Central Park Conservancy completed a complex renovation. Much of the hard work is out of sight: new drainage and irrigation systems, specially engineered soil and grass. But the gardeners assigned to take care of the new Great Lawn are evidence of a commitment to keep it great.

Today there are benches everywhere for spectators—of both people and sports. At the northeast corner, under a canopy of London plane trees, are four half-courts for basketball and two volleyball courts; a one-eighth mile track surrounds the courts.

Merely Wonderful

THE HARLEM MEER AND LANDSCAPE

East Side between 106th and 110th Streets

The 11-acre Harlem Meer (in Dutch "small sea") and its surrounding wooded landscape were the last parts of the Park to be built. The saying "Save the best for last," comes to mind when visitors experience this ruggedly beautiful setting. They can see swans and grebes leaving small jet wakes in the water. They can look south and see dramatic rock outcroppings angling sharply to the water, and then, with a simple turn of the head north, see the buildings of Harlem and watch traffic navigating Duke Ellington Circle.

The creation of the Harlem Meer was not, however, a straightforward process. In 1860 the creative genius of Olmsted's design skills were evident, but so, too, were his shortcomings as a manager. In *The Park and the People*, Roy Rosenzweig and Elizabeth Blackmar write that under Olmsted's watch, there were lengthy delays in Park construction and inconsistent oversight of Park expenditures. Olmsted insisted on staying in charge, however, saying, "No one but myself can understand at the present time, the true value or purpose of what is done on the Park. . . ." In spite of Olmsted's plea, the park commissioners turned to one of their own, placing Andrew Green, the board's comptroller, in charge. He saw to it that construction accelerated; he also completed financial negotiations for additional parkland between 106th and 110th Streets. These 65 acres constitute today's Harlem Meer landscape, which reflects Olmsted's design if not his construction management. Since Olmsted's plan was to retain the northern end's rugged topography, construction could proceed more quickly than in the southern Park, which had to be dramatically transformed to accommodate wholly new landscapes. A swamp became the 11-acre Harlem Meer, and the surrounding wooded areas came to include a planted ravine and rustic waterfall.

A 1940s reconstruction changed the existing soft grassy shoreline to a concrete and fenced edge. But in 1993, the Meer's shoreline was returned to Olmsted's original vision, with a miniature sandy beach added for whimsical effect. A cove in the southeast corner of the Meer has steps going down to the water's edge. There visitors can sit surrounded by native plants—roses, hydrangeas, pickerel weed, and irises—that spill down the slope to the water's edge. Surrounding the Meer are some of the Park's most impressive trees: oak, bald cypress, beech, and ginkgo.

The Meer and its landscapes today offer an amazing array of family-related activities: catch-and-release fishing; two playgrounds with water features; Park-related tours; exhibits and talks at the Charles A. Dana Discovery Center (see page 48); the nearby Conservatory Garden (see page 41); and Lasker Rink for skating or swimming (see page 134). Don't forget summer jazz and summer evening dancing on the terrace at 110th Street adjacent to the Dana Discovery Center.

A Point with a View

HERNSHEAD

**West Side between 75th and 76th Streets
On the Lake**

Hernshead is a miniature woodland landscape overlooking the Lake. The name "Hernshead" was derived from the shape of the prominent bedrock outcrop that punctuates the end of this small peninsula. To Olmsted and Vaux, its shape resembled the head of a heron ("hern" in its British translation). Olmsted lavished horticultural attention on this site, first with a grove of London plane trees and then with a variety of herbaceous plants and shrubs. Spring is Hernshead's season with blooming azaleas, Virginia bluebells, Dutchman's breeches, and daffodils. Violets add diminutive dots of color amid the

unfurling fern fronds. Most striking of all, in late June, is the copse of flowering white mountain laurel—a rare sight in Central Park.

A narrow pathway through the woods ends at a filigreed, cast-iron structure called The Ladies' Pavilion. Located originally at Columbus Circle on the site of the Maine Monument and intended to serve as a bus shelter, it was moved to Hernshead sometime after 1912. Like many of the Victorian vintage structures in the Park, it has elaborate ornamental detailing requiring consistent maintenance; the good news is that restoration is in the works, with plans for ongoing care. The Ladies' Pavilion provides a "time past" setting for admiring the vista of the Lake.

The Lake

Mid-Park between 71st and 78th Streets

"**B**elieve me, my young friend, there is nothing—absolutely nothing—half so much worth doing as simply messing about in boats," said Water Rat in *The Wind in the Willows* by Kenneth Grahame. And the Lake in Central Park is the ideal place for such messing around.

At 20 acres, the Lake is Central Park's largest body of water, excluding the Reservoir. Because of the many twists and turns in its shoreline, however, it seems much larger. Olmsted and Vaux created the Lake out of a large swamp; they intended it to provide boating in the summer and ice skating in the winter. In December 1858, while the rest of Central Park was under construction, the Lake was opened for ice-skating. The opening happened to coincide with a long string of hard winters in the City and sparked an instant craze for the sport. According to one account in the Park's Annual Report, as many as 40,000 people skated on the Lake in one day. Nature couldn't always be counted on to satisfy the demand for good ice, so Wollman Rink (see page 134) was opened in 1954, and the Lake closed for skating.

Boating is another matter. In the 19th century you could enjoy boating without lifting a finger. "Call" boats came with a private boatman who would ferry you wherever you wanted to go on the Lake. In addition to six-seater call boats plying the water, "passage" boats—larger, canopied boats carrying twelve passengers—made a circuit of the Lake starting from Bethesda Terrace and stopping at five boat landings along the shore where passengers could embark or disembark. It cost a dime to ride the entire loop.

Today four of the wooden boat landings exist (although they've been rebuilt): one in Wagner's Cove, two along the western shoreline, and one along the Ramble shoreline by Bow Bridge. Now you must row yourself, however; a boat can be rented at Loeb Boathouse. You can even take a gondola ride—an original 19th-century offering that is still available today.

Most visitors are content, however, to circle the Lake on foot, following the pathways that wind along its shoreline, watching the Park's treeline shifting in its reflection.

Bowling on the Green

LAWN SPORTS CENTER
**West Side between 69th and 70th Streets
Open May 1—October 1**

NEW YORK CROQUET CLUB (NYCC)
**Membership: $200/year with a one-time initiation
fee (includes dues, Park's permit, and membership
in the U.S. Croquet Association)
Information: 212-369-7949**

NEW YORK LAWN BOWLING CLUB
**Membership: $80/year (includes dues and Park's
permit) • Information: 212-289-3245**

Two handkerchief-sized, manicured lawns are the sites for croquet and lawn bowling in Central Park. Croquet began as an afternoon game for men and women to play together at the court of Louis the XIV of France. Some historians date its earliest antecedents to French shepherds who invented the game using their crooks and fieldstones. The game migrated to England and Ireland and was eventually exported to America about the time Central Park was undergoing construction. Although there was constant debate from the beginning about the kinds of recreation appropriate for the Park, croquet, with its portable, discreet equipment and small number of players, was clearly an acceptable option.

In spite of its 19th-century popularity, the first formal

croquet club in America, Central Park's New York Croquet Club, wasn't organized until 1966. The other traditional Park lawn sport is lawn bowling, which in one form or another, is one of the oldest games in the world. It is a close cousin to the Italian bocci, and the French *boule*. Lawn bowling in New York dates back to the time when the Dutch played bowls on a small patch of lawn behind the green in New Amsterdam. Today that lawn is part of Bowling Green Park in lower Manhattan. The Dutch colonial administrator, Peter Minuit, was one of the club's founding members. Bowling on the Green, as the sport is sometimes called, was organized in Central Park in 1926.

Lawn bowling and croquet are both sports of skill and style (players wear white), not strength. As with all sports in Central Park, these two make for great watching, as well as participating. The Croquet Club has free, Tuesday-night clinics and summer weekend tournaments. The New York Lawn Bowling Club offers free instruction by appointment and Tuesday, Thursday, and weekend club games.

Row, Row, Row Your Boat

LOEB BOATHOUSE

**East Side between 74th and 75th Streets
Park View at the Boathouse
Open for lunch noon to 4:30 pm
(from 11 am on weekends)
Dinner 5:30—10 pm
Main courses: $17—$24
Reservations: 212-517-2233**

**Bike Rental: March to October 9 am—5 pm
Approximate price per hour:
$6 for a children's bike; $14 for a tandem.
ID required.
Information: 212-861-4137**

**Row Boat Rental: Mid-April—mid-October 10 am to
one hour before dusk.
Price per hour: $10 with a $30 refundable deposit.
Information: 212-517-2233**

**Gondola Rental: March—mid-October 5:30—10 pm
(and for all catered events)
Price per half-hour: $30 (gondola seats six)
Reservations are strongly suggested.
Information: 212-517-2233**

With their 1858 landscaping plan under construction, Frederick Law Olmsted and Calvert Vaux began adding architectural features to their Park design. Around 1874, Vaux designed a two-story boathouse at the eastern end of the Lake. Here visitors could purchase refreshments, take boat rides, and watch other boats. After this wooden Victorian structure with a sloping mansard roof burned down, the current Loeb Boathouse took its place in the 1950s.

Today at the Boathouse visitors can enjoy a meal in any season, with overhead heating helping to extend as long as possible the pleasure of dining on the deck overlooking the Lake. More informal snacks are available on the outside terrace across from the bicycle-rental concession. At Loeb you can also rent rowboats or take a ride in an authentic Venetian gondola. This is more than a ride, it is an event—with luck, your gondolier might just break into song at some point during the trip.

To the west of the Boathouse entrance, at the entrance to the Ramble, is a small, wire-fenced area where the Conservancy, along with volunteers, is experimenting with growing wildflowers that attract butterflies. To date, 26 species of butterfly have been spotted. July and August are the best times to butterfly-watch.

Visitors also come to the Boathouse to record their observations of birds and other Park wildlife in the Bird Register. This unprepossessing 2-inch loose-leaf notebook, kept in the Boathouse, documents the incredible compendium of wildlife in the Park. Birders record birds seen or heard or document a small wildlife drama witnessed in one of the Park's landscapes.

Many Central Park birders make entries—in fact there is at least one entry for every day in 1998. On December 12, 1998, former President Jimmy Carter and his wife Rosalyn wrote, "Enjoyed [the book] *Red-tails in Love*—we've been birdwatchers for the past 10 years in about 15 nations and in a number of states. Glad to know the red-tails were seen yesterday. Have about 750 birds on our list. Hope to come back to Central Park and will." Birding aficionados report that 750 birds is an exceptional amount!

Some entries provide surprising information to birders. For example, the sighting of two snow geese at the Harlem Meer is rare for this area. And a growing number and variety of red-headed woodpeckers are being spotted on the west side of the Great Lawn. Some birds inspire nicknames—such as LEO, the long-eared owl that has returned the last four years to a Norway spruce at Cedar Hill, and Pale Male of Marie Winn's *Red-Tails in Love.*

Visitors should feel free to enter their observations and be part of this Central Park tradition.

Buskers and Skaters

THE MALL CONCERT GROUND

Mid-Park between 69th and 72nd Streets

The Concert Ground occupied a central place in Olmsted and Vaux's formal plan for Central Park; it was the point at which the Mall and Bethesda Terrace met. Perhaps Olmsted and Vaux envisioned New Yorkers promenading up the Mall, stopping occasionally to socialize as they proceeded to the Concert Ground. There the music would lift their minds and spirits from daily worries and prepare them for the inspiration that nature would provide in the views from Bethesda Terrace.

An ornate, cast-iron Bandstand originally stood to the side of the Concert Ground. Surrounding the Bandstand were urns and filigreed metal bird cages, ornamental drinking fountains, and display fountains—all

contributing to the effect of an overstuffed Victorian parlor. Vaux designed benches (similar to the ones there today) for resting, especially necessary since people tended to dress in their finest for Park concerts. Once concerts became established, a more casual attitude began to prevail. Commissioners allowed people to sit on the grass for concerts; families brought children and even left while concerts were still in progress. Historians Roy Rosenzweig and Elizabeth Blackmar quote a *New York Times* reporter of the day complaining that the "hedges of society for the time being are let down." He was confirmed in his indignation when "a gentleman in a seedy coat" blew cigar smoke in his face at one concert. It was a classic Central Park debate: how will the greatest of public spaces accommodate the public for whom it was designed?

To provide a shady overlook for the concert ground, Olmsted and Vaux perched a Wisteria Pergola on a high ridge to the east of the original bandshell. Although partially obscured by today's Naumburg Bandshell, the Pergola remains a cool refuge from summer sun, its gnarled wisteria vines woven over the years into a latticework roof, and the springtime wisteria providing aromatic pale lavender blossoms. The Naumburg Bandshell was built in 1923 to replace the earlier cast-iron bandstand. In 1923, the concert ground was enlarged, and the gilded birdcages and fountains were replaced with pavement.

Today there are nonamplified concerts at the Naumburg Bandshell. Summerstage, on the Rumsey Playfield behind the Wisteria Pergola, offers a variety of jazz and multicultural performances throughout the summer.

See and Be Seen

THE MALL OR
LITERARY WALK

East Side, Mid-Park between 66th and 69th Streets

The Mall and Bethesda Fountain are the only existing formal elements in Olmsted and Vaux's design for Central Park. They acknowledged the public's need for a place to socialize; they knew that a "grand promenade" was an "essential feature of a metropolitan park." But Olmsted and Vaux wanted to satisfy that need without compromising the primacy of the Park's natural features. They felt that the "hall of reception" (or Mall) must be secondary to the natural view, in this case of the Lake and the Ramble.

Flanking the 40-foot-wide Mall are quadruple rows of American elms. The elm was one of Olmsted's favorite trees and provides, as he envisioned, a living cathedral ceiling high over the walkway. The Mall is breathtaking in any season. In the springtime, the sun through the translucent leaves seems to tint the atmosphere a lime green. As the canopy matures over the summer, it creates a cool, dense shade for the landscape below. When October's and November's yellow and gold leaves fall, they reveal the bold architecture of the trees' skeletons. A fresh winter snow creates a lace veil in the black-and-white tree branches.

The Mall is sometimes referred to as "Literary Walk." Fearing that increasing requests to install sculpture throughout the Park would change its naturalistic character, Olmsted proposed in 1873 that the Mall be the designated location for sculpture. Over a short period of time representations of the following literary and historical figures were installed: *William Shakespeare* (by John Quincy Adams Ward, dedicated in 1872), *Christopher Columbus* (by Jeronimo Suñol, dedicated in 1894), *Sir Walter Scott* (by Sir John Steell, dedicated in 1872), *Robert Burns* (by James Wilson Alexander MacDonald, dedicated in 1877). Three other sculptures of outstanding individuals complete the selection: *Samuel F. B. Morse* (by Byron M. Picket, dedicated in 1871), *Victor Herbert* (by Edmond T. Quinn, 1927), and *Ludwig Van Beethoven* (by Henry

Bearer, 1884). Composers Herbert and Beethoven are near the Mall concert ground, site of the original Central Park Bandshell, and now of the Naumburg Bandshell and Summerstage at Rumsey Playing Field.

Historians Margot Gayle and Michele Cohen describe two other sculptures in the Mall area worthy of note, each eliciting divergent critical response in their time. The first is The *Indian Hunter* by John Quincy Adams Ward (dedicated in 1869) which helped to establish Ward as a leading post–Civil War sculptor. Critics felt a harmonious connection with the Park in Ward's observation of nature and in his focus on a truly American subject. Christophe Eratin's *Eagles and Prey* (dedicated in 1863) did not fare as well. Park commissioners thought the naturalistic theme would be highly appropriate for a Park setting. But noted 19th-century critic Clarence Cook disagreed, saying in 1869 that such wild, exotic depictions (in this case, two birds of prey attacking a goat trapped between two rocks) did not fit in with "the tranquil rural beauty of the park scenery. . . ." Such sculpture flew in the face, as it were, of the nobler purpose of both art and the Park's design, felt Cook.

Finally, one little-known fact: at the southernmost end of the Mall is the only tribute in Central Park to Frederick Law Olmsted. The Olmsted Flowerbed, recently beautified with seasonal pansies, impatiens, and flowing groundcover, is a memorial garden surrounded by American elms. Its elegant but naturalistic plantings, both annual and perennial, offer year-round color and texture for the delight of Park visitors.

MERCHANTS' GATE

**Columbus Circle at Central Park South
and Central Park West**

Merchants' Gate at Columbus Circle is one of Central Park's four main entrances along Central Park South. These entrances, the first the visitor would encounter in the 1880s when traveling north from densely populated southern Manhattan, were named "to extend each citizen a rightful welcome." In addition to Merchants' Gate, there was Artisans' Gate at Central Park South and Seventh Avenue; Artists' Gate at Central Park South and Sixth Avenue, and Scholars' Gate at Grand Army Plaza (see pg 57). Fighting back calls for elaborate entrances (such as a dramatic classical design proposed by popular Beaux-Arts architect William Morris Hunt), Olmsted and Vaux prevailed with unobtrusive openings that punctuated the low sandstone wall around the Park. Eventually most of the 18 original entrances recognized professions.

But at Merchants' Gate—as at Sixth Avenue and Grand Army Plaza—monuments to battles or generals were added over time to adorn the plain entrances. The professions took second place to military memorials. Generals José Martí, José de San Martín, and Simón Bolívar are astride spirited horses at Sixth Avenue, and a weary General Sherman pauses at Grand Army Plaza. But Merchants' Gate at Columbus Circle boasts the most imposing monument of the lot. It is a colossal 1913 Beaux-Arts monument built to commemorate the sinking of the battleship Maine in 1898; there remains debate over what triggered the explosion but there's no doubt that it precipitated the Spanish-American War (April–July 1898). The monument itself is a massive 44-foot lime-

stone pylon. Crowning the pylon is a gilded bronze sculpture of *Columbia Triumphant* in a seashell chariot pulled by three seahorses. Churning through the gilt waves, *Columbia* signifies the United States' dominance of the seas. Supporting the rightness of that claim are the allegorical figures at the pylon's base: Victory, Peace, Courage, Fortitude, and Justice. The monument not only salutes the Americans killed in the war, but also announces the country's new status as a world power. To spread that message, skillful promoters paid for the monument by collecting pennies and nickels donated by school children after the Spanish-American War.

The monument is clearly the dominant presence at the Park entrance. But visitors should also take time to admire the restored plaza where it sits. In the pavement is a spiral basketweave pattern of bluestone and granite in various shades of pink, blue, and gray. To define the plaza area and separate it from the Park there is a low marble wall behind the monument at just the right height for sitting down. In clement weather there are two green, Italian, wrought-iron–style kiosks on the plaza in keeping with its Columbus Circle location. The concessionaires provide several tables and chairs and offer Italian coffees and desserts. Just the thing to do while pondering the course of world history.

Art in the Park

METROPOLITAN MUSEUM OF ART

Fifth Avenue at 82nd Street
Suggested donation: $8 adults; $4 seniors and students
Open Tuesday–Sunday 9:30 am–5:15 pm
Evening hours on Friday and Saturdays until 8:45 pm
Information: 212-535-7710

The original Metropolitan Museum of Art was a gothic-style brick building designed by Calvert Vaux and Jacob Wrey Mould. *The Park and the People* reports that when the Museum opened in Central Park in 1880, some critics described that first building as a "cross between a train station and a packing house." They believed the City's future great art museum should be an imposing architectural statement; they did not subscribe to Vaux's theory that all architecture in the Park should be subordinate to the landscape. Over the years, the Museum added new wings and new floors, expanding to cover today's 13 acres. As the Museum grew, it literally swallowed the original structure, building around and over it. Visitors can see a portion of the original building's brick wall left exposed in the Lehman Wing. In 1895, Richard Morris Hunt built the first of many additions; his grand Beaux-Arts wing reoriented the Museum so that it faced away from the Park toward Fifth Avenue. In 1906,

McKim, Mead, and White expanded the Museum in their noted classical style, which defines the building's façade today.

Before entering the Museum, walk north the length of the building. In good weather, there are likely to be artists displaying and selling photographs, oil paintings (some "custom-made" on the spot, others presumably the product of longer efforts), and Russian nesting dolls. Passing the front steps, check the three-story colorful banners—often works of art in themselves—that announce the new exhibits. At the end of the building take the first path west into the Park past the slanted glass wall of the Temple of Dendur. The view will vary with the time of day; in full daylight the clear glass panels reflect the Park, much like a giant mirrored mosaic. At night with a navy blue sky, the Temple, illuminated inside, seems to glow with its own inner light. Continue your circle around the

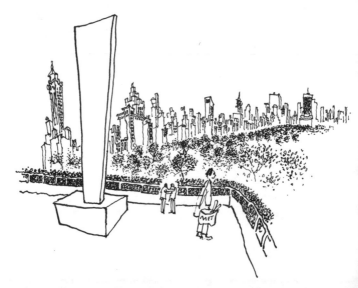

Museum bearing to the left. Duck your head under the low branches of cherry trees that have pink pompoms of blossoms in the spring. Continue walking, and the *Obelisk* (Cleopatra's Needle, see page 96) will be on the right, beside Greywacke Arch, where a jazz saxophonist sometimes plays, enjoying the acoustics of the brick archway. Another turn to the left winds past the playground where Paul Manship's welcoming sculpture of three bears greets children. A left turn again puts you on Fifth Avenue, ready to experience the extraordinary collections that make the Metropolitan one of the premier art museums in the world.

A Star-Spangled Setting

MILITARY FORTIFICATIONS

Between 96th and 110th Streets

Every acre of New York City has a story to tell. Central Park is no exception, offering history predating its own 140 years. Much of this rich pre-Park history is the result of the rugged topography that defines what we now call the Upper Park landscape. Visitors to the Harlem Meer, the Ravine, and the Great Hill, can step back in time to the days of the American Revolution or the War of 1812.

The steep bluffs bordering the southern shoreline of the Harlem Meer were a significant military site during both wars. From the bluffs the northern part of Manhattan was visible, as was the Long Island Sound. The major road linking Manhattan with cities on the mainland to the north went through a break in the bluffs that was named McGown's Pass after the owners of a nearby tavern. In 1776, British and Hessian troops sealed off lower Manhattan from colonial armies by controlling the pass and defending it through a series of fortifications. British and Hessian troops occupied the fortifications along the bluffs until the end of the Revolutionary War. Camps for the soldiers were erected on what is now the Great Hill and the North and East Meadows.

Almost 40 years later, in 1814, the Americans

returned to these very sites to rebuild the strongholds against a possible British invasion from the north through the Long Island Sound. The old British fortifications were hastily rebuilt by volunteer citizens. The fort to the west of McGown's Pass was named Nutter's Battery after the owner of a nearby farm. Fort Clinton to the east of the pass was named after Mayor DeWitt Clinton, and a higher bluff to the south was called Fort Fish after the chairman of the City's Committee of Defense. Some 1,600 New York State militia spent the fall of 1814 at McGown's Pass, but peace arrived and not a shot was fired there.

One additional fortification from the War of 1812 still stands as a remnant in the Park—Block House #1. It is a stone shell, located north of the Great Hill in the North Woods. Originally it was to be a two-story bunker, with a revolving turret for a cannon.

Perhaps the most dramatic piece of history regarding the area has to do with George Washington. Defeated in the Battle of Brooklyn in late August 1776, the American troops were retreating to a stronger position in northern Manhattan. On September 15th the British landed on the East River at

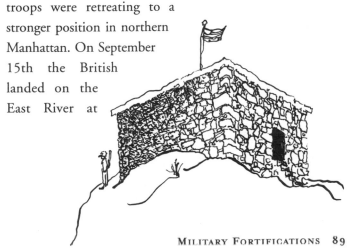

Kip's Bay, nearly cutting off part of General George Washington's army. Washington, headquartered near 160th Street, heard the shelling and galloped through McGown's Pass on his way toward the battle. Washington arrived in time to lead his troops to safety up the West Side of the island to a position just beyond Central Park's northern boundary. The next day the colonists fought and won the Battle of Harlem Heights, pushing the British back into their encampments in Central Park, which the British and the Hessians held for the next seven years.

A Rustic Oasis

NATURALISTS' WALK

West Side between 77th and 81st Streets

This newly restored and varied landscape is directly across from the American Museum of Natural History. A new Park entrance in the Central Park West perimeter wall facing the Museum welcomes tourists, local residents, and school children into the Park. Perhaps the liveliest Naturalists' Walk users are the school children. After studying the Museum's vast collections and touring the new Hall of Biodiversity, they stream out of the Museum past orange buses to explore nature in living color. The landscape was restored with that educational connection in mind: there is even a rustic outdoor "classroom"

near a large boulder outcrop in the center of the landscape, where students can gather with their teachers and sit on split-log benches.

A network of soft-surface paths radiates outward from rustic benches at the Park entrance. Visitors can follow one pathway north, which leads past massive royal paulownia trees with huge, grapelike leaves; along that path are outcrops of Manhattan schist, the bedrock of the island's skyscrapers.

Another path dips south into a valley landscape with a broad, grassy meadow. Just like Sheep Meadow and Cedar Hill, it is a perfect spot for lolling and reading and soaking up the sun. Adding to the restful setting is a stream on the far eastern edge of the Lawn; it flows from a rocky grotto, under a rustic wooden bridge, and into a thicket of small trees. The stream is a vestige of the Ladies' Pond, a long-gone area of the Lake set aside for women to practice their ice skating skills in privacy. Native plants chosen for their appeal to butterflies and birds cover the slopes around the grotto. There is red-osier dogwood with bright, shiny red stems that stand out in wintertime. The red chokeberry has red fruit in fall and winter and white flowers in May. Adding to the palette is black-eyed Susan, a summer-blooming yellow flower with a black center. Joe-Pye-weed, a plant as dramatic in color as it is odd in name, has a purplish flower and can be six-feet tall.

The southern border of Naturalists' Walk is Eaglevale Bridge, a massive gneiss (granitelike rock) and ashlar (squared masonry) arch built at the turn-of-the-century to provide another entrance to the Park drive for westside residents. This is the only bridge in the Park with a double arch. Originally one arch was a water connection for the second lobe of the Ladies' Pond and the other combined the bridge trail and a pathway. There are twin American elms on the south side of the bridge.

Walking south under Eaglevale Bridge the visitor comes to Azalea Walk—a colorful springtime variety of azaleas and rhododendrons. Azalea varieties range from the smooth azalea with white flowers to the Delaware Valley white to the Pinkster flowers and Swamp azalea, also with white flowers. The Carolina rhododendron adds pale rose flowers to the mix, as does the aptly-named Rosebay rhododendron. And it is a short walk to Strawberry Fields (see page 120), where there are wild strawberries! There also is American holly at Strawberry Fields on the large main lawn; it has lustrous green foliage with bright red berries, especially appealing to birds. The woodland walk that winds through the Strawberry Fields landscape is bordered by ferns, snakeroot, witchhazel (with yellow flowers in the fall and early spring), and black locust, with white May flowers that give off a honeysuckle-like fragrance.

Batter Up!

NORTH MEADOW

Mid-Park between 97th and 102nd Streets

NORTH MEADOW RECREATION CENTER

Mid-Park at 97th Street

The North Meadow, at 50 acres, is the Park's largest grassy space. The Great Lawn (which was not part of Olmsted and Vaux's original plan, see page 63), shares its 55 acres with Turtle Pond, the wooded Arthur Ross Pinetum, tree-planted borders, and a playground for basketball and volleyball. The North Meadow, like the 14-acre Great Lawn oval today, is punctuated only by the clay fans of ballfields. At this writing, the 12 fields for baseball, softball, and soccer are under restoration and slated to open for permitted use in the spring of 2000.

Park officials formally approved North Meadow for baseball in the 1870s. But the outfitting of the fields came much later. During Robert Moses's first year as Parks Commissioner in 1934, *The New York Times Magazine* described the extensive "plowing, seeding, planting, and replanting" at North Meadow to create new athletic fields that gave "the grass effect of a big-college football field or the polo field of a country club." Formal ballfield diamonds had come to stay.

The North Meadow Recreation Center, which borders the Meadow, is a relative newcomer to the Park in its current use. Built originally as stables, it was converted to a recreational facility in the early 1990s and underwent a second refurbishment in 1998. The

exterior of the building was preserved to protect its Landmark status, but the interior has a cushioned exercise floor, high ceilings, and a community room with computer stations. The computers are part of the Center's focus on fitness and general health, in addition to sports. Animated CD-Rom programs teach children basic anatomy and wellness principles; a cocky three-dimensional skeleton chatters his way through each lesson. The Central Park Conservancy staff uses a variety of approaches to encourage self-esteem among the elementary, middle school, and high school age students who take these courses. One instructor may teach basketball refereeing skills and another may teach wall climbing on one of two climbing walls (one indoor and one outdoor.) All the courses are offered free of charge and are coordinated with local schools and community board organizations.

And then there's just, plain play. The Center offers Field Day kits on loan. With a photo ID, a visitor can borrow a kit with a variety of balls, bats, hula-hoops, Frisbees, and jump ropes.

Cleopatra's Needle

THE OBELISK

East Side at 81st Street

The oldest man-made object in Central Park, by a long shot, is the Obelisk, located directly behind the Metropolitan Museum of Art. Nicknamed Cleopatra's Needle in the 19th century, the dedication of the obelisk in fact has nothing to do with Cleopatra, but was a self-commissioned tribute to Egypt's Thutmosis III (an accurate attribution, but clearly without the popular appeal of the Queen of the Nile). The Obelisk was erected in Heliopolis around 1500 BC, was moved to Alexandria, and from there to the United States in 1879. The Khedive of Egypt (who governed as a viceroy of the Sultan of Turkey between 1879 and 1914) offered it to the United States in the hope of stimulating trade between the two countries.

Moving the Obelisk from Alexandria, Egypt, to Central Park was a feat second only to its original construction. Imagine moving a 71-foot, 244-ton granite needle, first from vertical to horizontal, then into the hold of a ship, across the Mediterranean Sea and over the storm-tossed Atlantic Ocean, without breakage. It took four months just to bring it from the banks of the Hudson River to the Park! The final leg of the journey was made across a specially built trestle bridge from Fifth Avenue to its new home on Greywacke Knoll. The site, just across the drive from the then newly-built Metropolitan Museum of Art, was quietly chosen over such other worthy competitors as Columbus Circle and Union Square.

You realize the massive scale of the Obelisk only when you stand right at its base, supported at each corner by bronze replicas of sea crabs crafted by the Romans (and on display in the Sackler Wing of the Metropolitan Museum); one crab alone weighs approximately 900 pounds. A recently restored plaza around the Obelisk has benches for admiring the Obelisk's design, manufacture, and inscription. Surrounding the plaza are Japanese yews, magnolias, and crab apples. Visitors can sit on the surrounding benches and ponder the passing of history or simply enjoying the passing of the seasons.

Child Required

PLAYGROUNDS

There are 21 playgrounds in Central Park, each one functioning like a small village where local families can meet, socialize, and make new friends. The playgrounds are

all near the Park perimeter, just a short walk from the surrounding City streets. Over time, each has developed its own style and fan club. They are continually being enhanced, with new state-of-the-art safety features and replacements for heavily used equipment. Here is a listing from north to south, west side to east side.

West Side Playgrounds (in order from north to south):

- **Playground at Central Park West and 110th Street**—Colorful pipe-frame equipment, sandbox, water-spray feature, and tot swings.

- **Playground at West 100th Street**—Wood-and pipe-frame equipment with rope swing, tree house, and water spray.

- **Rudin Family Playground at West 97th Street**—Colorful pipe-frame equipment, tire swings, tot swings, sandbox, and water spray. Wisteria pergola in the center for shady seating.

- **Wild West Playground at West 83rd Street**—Sand surface under wood-play equipment, tot and older child swings, and water spray.
- **Safari Playground at West 91st Street**—Thirteen hippopotamuses in various states of submersion. One spouts water. Two tree houses and a canoe to go on "safari."
- **Abraham and Joseph Spector Playground at West 86th Street**—Wood-and pipe-frame play equipment in sand area, tot swings, water spray, and rope swing.
- **Rochelle and Arthur Belfer Playground at West 84th Street**—Colorful pipe-frame play equipment in boatlike shapes, tot swings, water spray, sandbox, tot seesaw, and spring toys. Some equipment is wheelchair accessible. The playground has a nautical theme in keeping with nearby Mariners' Gate.
- **Diana Ross Playground at West 81st Street**—Wood play equipment on sand surface and water spray. Named for the pop singer who helped fund its construction.
- **Adventure Playground at West 67th Street**—First adventure playground in Central Park and recently restored. Timber pyramid and play equipment. Water spray and channel.
- **Tot Playground at West 67th Street**—Colorful pipe-frame equipment for tots. Sandbox and tot swings. Smallest playground in Central Park.
- **Heckscher Playground between 61st and 63rd Streets Mid-Park**—Largest playground in Central Park with

full range of play equipment.

- **Pinetum Playground in the northwest corner of the Great Lawn at 85th Street**—A picnic area with toddler and junior swings and a chin-up bar.

East Side Playgrounds (in order from south to north):

- **Billy Johnson Playground, "Rustic Playground," at East 67th Street**—tot swings, water spray, and sandbox. Has rustic wood features. Long, curved, granite slide. A big hit with the toddler crowd.
- **Harriet and Robert Heilbrunn Playground at East 72nd Street**—Under renovation at this writing.

- **James Michael Levin Playground at East 76th Street**—Colorful pipe-frame equipment, tot swings, sand play area, and the *Sophie Irene Loeb Fountain*, designed by Frederick George Richard Roth in 1936. The concrete fountain's centerpiece features reliefs of figures from *Alice's Adventures in Wonderland*: Alice, the Duchess, the Cheshire Cat, the Mad Hatter, the White Rabbit, the Griffon, a Kneeling Page, the Queen and the King of Hearts.

- **Pat Hoffman Friedman Playground at East 79th Street**—Pipe-frame play equipment, sandbox, and water spray. Paired with Paul Manship's *Group of Bears* sculpture.
- **Ancient Playground at East 84th Street**—Adventure play pyramids and wood play equipment. Water spray, tire swings, and a separate tot sandbox area. Restrooms are available.
- **Playground at East 97th Street**—Colorful pipe-frame play equipment, tree house, tire swings, tot swings, sandbox and sand table.
- **Robert Bendheim Playground at East 100th Street**—Colorful pipe-frame play equipment, tot swings, sandbox, and sand table, and water spray spiral. The playground is specifically designed for use by able-bodied and physically challenged children.
- **Bernard Family Playground at East 108th Street**—Colorful pipe-frame play equipment, tot swings, and water spray.
- **Playground at 110th Street near the Charles A. Dana Discovery Center**—Wood play equipment and water spray.

A Welcome Mat: Olmsted Style

THE POND

Central Park South between
Fifth and Sixth Avenues

T he southeast corner of Central Park was from its inception, and continues to be today, the most heavily used Park entrance. Fully half of all Park visitors enter by way of Grand Army Plaza (see page 57). In the 19th century it was the first destination of a carriage ride north from the growing City to the Park; in the late 20th century it offers office workers from surrounding buildings and foot-weary tourists a respite. Horse-drawn carriages exit the Park at the southeast corner and wait in line along Central Park South—the horses munching oats and the drivers calling out for fares.

Olmsted and Vaux intended the Pond land-scape, just inside the entrance, to welcome visitors and offer an instant haven from the City. The comma-shaped Pond is situated below street level, which has the effect of muting the urban cacophony and creating a surpris-

ing calm. Simple grass lawns and pathways lined with benches surround the Pond. The gracefully shaped Gapstow Bridge, made from Manhattan schist (the local bedrock) arches over the northeast end of the Pond, framing the picturesque scene. Visitors can also visit the Cop Cot, Scottish for "little house on the crest of the hill," perched on a large rock outcrop at the Sixth Avenue entrance and providing a view of the Pond below. The Cop Cot is also the Park's largest rustic wood structure.

Visitors may notice a fenced-in wooded area jutting into the Pond. Originally called the Promontory, it is now the Hallett Nature Sanctuary (Bird Sanctuary). It was designated a wildlife sanctuary in 1934 in honor of George Hervey Hallett, Jr., an ardent birdwatcher, naturalist, and civic leader. It is comprised of four acres open only for special tours and is the smallest of the Park's woodlands.

The Wind and the Willows

THE POOL

West Side, between 100th and 103rd Streets

The Pool is easily one of the most idyllic landscapes in Central Park. All the elements of Olmsted and Vaux's original design have endured here and matured. Few landscapes in the Park have the renewing spiritual quality of the Pool. The grassy banks, the willows bent over the water, the rushing sounds of a nearby waterfall all make it a unique spot for contemplation or meditation in the midst of the bustling City.

Southwest of the Pool is a naturalistic boulder grotto where a stream ripples forth and flows into the Pool. This little grotto is a perfect reminder that Central Park is entirely man-made: behind the boulder is a 48-inch pipe that brings fresh water from the Reservoir one-half mile south to the Pool. This conduit is, amazingly, the main source of water that keeps the Pool, the Loch, and the Harlem Meer filled and the cascades in between running.

The most dramatic cascade, recalling mountain hikes or trips to northern New York State's Adirondack forests, is by the bridge at the northeast corner of the Pool. Here water pours over the rocky man-made dam to create a 14-foot high-waterfall called The First Cascade. At the cascade's base the stream called the Loch begins; it flows under Glenspan Arch and into the wooded Ravine. Here the landscape changes from the romantic Pool with its willows and red maple to a loamy-smelling pathway beneath a canopy of oaks, elms, and maples.

THE RAMBLE

Mid-Park between 73rd and 79th Streets

No part of the Park has so varied or so intricate a landscape as the Ramble and no part shows off more dramatically the landscape design skills of Frederick Law Olmsted. The Ramble is a 38-acre "wild garden" (in Olmsted's words) with rocky outcrops, secluded glades, and a tumbling stream called The Gill. The Park's designers literally sculpted the Ramble out of a wooded hillside. One of the first parts of the Park to be built, the Ramble is—except for its bedrock platform—totally artificial. Even the water running in the Gill is turned on and off with a water tap.

The purpose of the Ramble was to invite the visitor to stroll (hence the name) and to discover serendipitously forest gardens rich with plantings from the Adirondack or Appalachian Mountain ranges. Meandering paths would lure the urban explorer away from the City and present opportunities to experience nature, both plant and animal.

Over time, the Ramble has become the epicenter of birding activity in the Park—as many as 230 species of birds have been spotted. It is an ideal sanctuary, its hundreds of trees, shrubs, and wildflowers interspersed with glades along the northern border. The Lake wraps around the Ramble's southern and western borders creating cover and peninsulas that offer great bird watching.

The Ramble's open woodland thickets, for example, harbor more than 20 species of warblers that fly in during spring and fall migration, in April/May and September/October, respectively. Given its topography and location on the Atlantic flyway (the migration route that birds follow during the spring and fall), the Ramble has been rated one of the top 15 birdwatching sites in the entire United States.

Visitors who feel the historical names of Park sites—the Lake, the Pool, East Meadow, for example—are a bit plain will appreciate the colorful nicknames of Ramble sites. Christened by birders to clue in fellow birders, they include: the Oven, Willow Rock, Bank Rock Bay, the Humming Tombstone (a granite-covered electrical control box for pathway lights that actually hums), and the Riviera.

The popularity of the Ramble combined with its intricate landscape designs of pathways and plantings have made it vulnerable to heavy use. After thorough study and consultation with environmental groups, a

restoration plan is underway; today's visitor can see signs of its progress. The goal of the woodlands restoration and management program is to gradually restore the forest floor and control off-path trampling and bike riding. To view the restoration in progress, head toward the stone arch on the western edge of the Ramble. The fenced-off landscapes have been resoiled and planted with native plants such as arrowwood viburnam, summersweet, and shrub dogwood. Educational signs give more information about the program.

Trees dating from the Ramble's planting now populate this woodland. One of the most famous—a tupelo—is located in the meadow directly south of Belvedere Castle. In the fall, its leaves turn a brilliant ruby red. Some visitors have nicknamed it the "squirrel house" because of the number of squirrel nests in the canopy; they are best seen in the winter without the camouflage of leaves. Be on the lookout for swamp white, red, and pin oaks, and tulip trees. Also look for the red maple and sophora trees surrounding Azalea Pond, in the heart of the Ramble.

Although large wild animals like deer, wolves, and black bear left the Park long ago, the Ramble does have one panther. *Still Hunt*, the name of the bronze sculpture created by Edward Kemeys, crouches—tail in mid-twitch—on the edge of the Ramble on an outcrop overlooking the east drive between 76th and 77th Streets.

THE RAVINE

Mid-Park between 102nd and 106th Streets

Visitors will feel they have been transported to the Adirondacks, but they have simply come to a piece of man-made scenery where Nature rules. Under the forest canopy of the Ravine, the City's skyline is nowhere to be seen and the continual din of traffic recedes against the rushing sound of a hidden waterfall and the chatter of birds.

The Ravine, the only stream valley in the Park, is part of the 90-acre woodland in the Upper Park called the North Woods. It is bounded to the north and south by two rustic arches called Huddlestone and Glenspan. The Loch, a stream that flows beside the pathway under both bridges, is dammed at several places to create the cascades you hear as you stroll through the Ravine.

Stop for a moment to study Huddlestone Arch. This picturesque piece of architecture was built without the help of mortar or metal supports. Constructed of immense boulders weighing from one to 20 tons and found near the site, it looks as though a natural cataclysm happened to deposit them in this form. One boulder, a 20-ton behemoth, was moved a short distance to form part of the base. How did they do it? The Park's Annual Report from 1858 tells us that Olmsted was authorized to employ house movers to move "rocks" whenever he thought it was advisable.

The northwest slope of the Ravine is a true deciduous forest of oak, hickory, maple, and ash. The forest floor is covered with leaf litter, dead wood, and herbaceous plants, such as white wood aster, Allegheny spurge, and woodland goldenrod. From the trail, visitors have a bird's-eye view of the central part of the Loch. Designed by Olmsted and Vaux as a long narrow lake (loch is the Scottish word for lake), it has over the past century reverted to its pre-Park form as a stream. The thickets growing on the islands of accumulated silt attract a wide variety of birds, sometimes including the rarely seen glossy ibis.

Another birding locale is the tall grass and wildflower meadow on the Ravine's southeastern slope. The meadow is at its most glorious in the late summer and fall. Coneflower, cup plant, and bee balm mixed in with a variety of goldenrods, asters, and native grasses set the hillside ablaze with color.

Water, Water Everywhere
THE RESERVOIR

Mid-Park between 85th and 96th Streets

The Reservoir is probably best known for the 1.58-mile track surrounding it and the thousands of runners who tone up there every day. The Reservoir itself (recently named the Jacqueline Kennedy Onassis Reservoir) contributes significantly to the environmental pleasure of the "run," particularly in the summer when water evaporation from its surface cools the surrounding air. As if this weren't enough, the track also boasts some of the best Park views of the New York City skyline.

The 106-acre water body, which holds a billion gallons of water, is the largest feature in the Park that is not under the actual jurisdiction of the Parks Department. Even the jogging track is the old access road for the Department of Environmental Protection to maintain the Reservoir. The

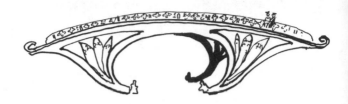

Reservoir was completed in 1862 while the Park was under construction. Although it no longer distributes fresh water to Manhattan residents, its overflow is critical for providing fresh water to the Pool, Loch, and Harlem Meer, the series of connecting water bodies in the northern part of the Park.

On your walk or run around the Reservoir take a moment to admire the three pedestrian cast-iron bridges that span the Bridle Trail. Originally known only by numbers 24, 27, and 28, the best known and most elegant is undoubtedly Bridge No. 28 (recently christened the Gothic Arch), just south of the Tennis Courts. Its silhouette suggests more lace cutout than bridge architecture.

Note also the three ornamental stone gatehouses designed by Calvert Vaux—two on the north and one on the southeast shore of the Reservoir—that house the equipment necessary to control water flow and treat the water. At the Reservoir's major entry at East 90th Street is the John Purroy Mitchel Monument, a curious terrace commemorating one of New York's youngest mayors, who served one term during 1914–1917. The gilded bust of Mitchel was created by Adolf Alexander Weinman and dedicated in 1926. Mitchel died in a plane crash while training as a WWI pilot. (One version of the story is that he forgot to buckle his seat belt and fell out of the plane.)

Runners' Gate, a more recent name for what was originally called Engineers' Gate, is the major entrance for the start and finish of the weekly races sponsored by the New York Road Runners Club. The NYRRC, founded in 1958 by Fred Lebow, organizes all running events in Central Park, including the New York City Marathon in November of each year. In 1998, over 32,000 runners participated, representing 113 countries from around the world.

Bird watchers also value the running track as a superb vantage point from which to spot birds in every season. They have sighted five different species of gulls and over 20 species of waterfowl, grebes, cormorants, and loons. Sightings are particularly rich during the winter, when many other birding spots are relatively inactive.

The Reservoir track is particularly delightful in the spring when the ornamental cherry trees are in bloom on the slopes below the track. The trees to the north and south of Purroy Mitchel Monument are probably some of the oldest ornamental cherry trees in the Park, some dating back to a gift from the nation of Japan in 1912 to commemorate the Hudson-Fulton Centennial.

No Lonesome Pines

ARTHUR ROSS PINETUM

Mid-Park between 84th and 86th Streets

That intoxicating scent of pine—coming as a surprise in the heart of Manhattan—signals the visitor has come to the Arthur Ross Pinetum. Created in 1971 by New York philanthropist Arthur Ross, this scientific collection of pine species contains the largest number of evergreens in the Park—more than 425 trees representing 27 species from around the world.

Evergreens played an important role in the original design of the Park. Olmsted and Vaux created a Winter Drive along the western carriage road from 102nd to

72nd Streets. Groupings of pines, spruces, and firs added color to the winter landscape and provided a backdrop for deciduous shrubs and oak, ash, and maple trees.

The most exotic part of the Pinetum collection is perhaps the western corner, with Swiss stone, Tahyosha, lacebark, and Swiss mountain pines all planted during the 1997 reconstruction of the Great Lawn. More well known are the varieties of white pine—the queen of the Adirondack forests in upstate New York—and the distinctive Himalayan pines with their bundles of long, light-green needles bending gracefully toward the earth.

Birdwatchers are fond of this area, especially in winter when migrating long-eared and saw-whet owls can be spotted sleeping during the day in the protective pine trees. A free walking tour available at Belvedere Castle (at the southern end of the Great Lawn) can help identify birds, trees, and walks of interest. There is also a free seasonal Pinetum tour, usually the first Sunday in December, ending at the Dairy with a Dixie-playing Santa Claus band and sugar cookies.

A Rose by Any Other Name

SHAKESPEARE GARDEN

West Side between 79th and 80th Streets

Shakespeare Garden, nestled amidst the Delacorte Theater, Belvedere Castle, and the Swedish Cottage, is an informal four-acre cottage garden nestled in a rocky hillside. The garden was dedicated to Shakespeare in 1916, the 300th anniversary of Shakespeare's death. Following a Victorian tradition, only flowers mentioned in Shakespeare's plays and poetry were planted in the garden.

After many years of neglect, the garden was completely reconstructed in 1987. Only the trees and a few existing shrubs were kept from the original plan. One tree that now shades the lower part of the garden is supposedly a graft of a white mulberry tree planted by Shakespeare's own hands at New Place, Stratford-on-Avon, in the year 1602. The cutting was sent to him by King James I in His Majesty's attempt to introduce silk culture into England. The lovely rustic wood seating deck under the canopy of the mulberry tree

is a perfect place to look closely at the garden details.

Planted on the steep slope of Vista Rock, the Garden's path twists and turns to its summit. Rustic benches punctuate the path and climbing roses intertwine the rustic wood fence that surrounds the entire Garden. Every season offers its different pleasures, but spring is the most tender. In March the hellebores, columbines, and Virginia bluebells are in full blossom. April and May offer daffodils, violets, and tulips with names such as Hearts Delight. The iris and the rose appear in late spring.

Summer greenery is more profuse, with herbs scenting the air and ferns, mallows, poppies, and black-eyed Susans in abundance. Asters, ornamental grasses, and broom sedges provide autumn color. Holly and Eastern hemlocks dominate in winter.

Visitors may see branches woven together to protect some of the more fragile plants. The gardener has taken inspiration for these tiny fences from medieval times and is recycling pruning leftovers. Scattered throughout the garden are bronze plaques that provide the Shakespearean quotation that inspired the planting.

For setting and mood, the Shakespeare Garden may be the perfect place for a pre-Delacorte Theater picnic.

Make Wool, Not War

SHEEP MEADOW

West Side, Mid-Park between 66th and 69th Streets
Open mid-April—mid-October
Dawn to dusk in fair weather

Sheep Meadow today is a 15-acre, lush, green mead-ow for relaxing and admiring one of New York City's greatest skyline views. But it began less placidly—at least in concept. One of the conditions for entries in the 1858 Central Park design competition was the inclusion of a parade ground for military drills. Historians Roy Rosenzweig and Elizabeth Blackmar write that Olmsted and Vaux included the parade ground in their design only reluctantly. The Park Commissioners were soon won over to their point of view, however, agreeing that military displays were perhaps not in keeping with the vision of a "people's park." To drive home the pastoral aspect of Central Park's design sensibility, Olmsted and Vaux accepted an alternative use: a sheepfold for 150 sheep.

The sheep and a shepherd were housed in a fanciful Victorian building—part of what is now the Tavern on the Green restaurant—on the western perimeter of the Park. Twice a day the shepherd stopped traffic on the west drive so that the flock could travel to and from their meadow. The rural idyll continued until the 1930s, when the flock was shipped out of the Park and the sheepfold became a restaurant. (We do not know if mutton was featured on the menu . . .)

In the 1960s and the 1970s the Sheep Meadow was the site of other gatherings: the 1969 moon-landing watch, hippie be-ins, large-scale concerts, and heavy sports use. Not surprisingly, Sheep Meadow was the candidate for one of the Park's first major landscape restorations in the 1980s. Events moved to nearby, more suitable or resilient locations. Sheep Meadow reopened in 1981 as a swath of green dedicated to sunbathers, picnickers, and kite flyers. Today, warm Sundays find New Yorkers with their newspapers, bagels, and designer coffee sitting cross-legged on fresh green grass.

On the northern edge of Sheep Meadow, just outside its fence, is Lilac Walk. Along the walk are 23 varieties of lilacs from around the world. The Center Drive, slightly further on, offers volleyball and the "skate circle"—the setting for serious roller-skating and disco-skating.

Imagine

STRAWBERRY FIELDS

West Side between 71st and 74th Streets

Imagine peace and quiet in Central Park's Garden of
Peace. In this tear-shaped landscape you can find both.
But first make a "pilgrim's progress" along with the bus-
loads of tourists that visit Strawberry Fields every day to the
black-and-white mosaic with the single word "IMAGINE"
in the center. Shaded by a grove of stately American elms,
the medallion is a reproduction of a mosaic from Pompeii
and is a gift of Naples, Italy. Hardly a day goes by without
some remembrance of John Lennon being placed upon
it—a rose, a poem, a candle, dried flowers. United by nos-
talgia, curiosity or a love for music, visitors come from

around the world—or from as close as the local west-side neighborhood.

Take a stroll down the hill past a bronze plaque that lists the 125 countries endorsing Strawberry Fields as a Garden of Peace. In 1981, after the assassination of former Beatle John Lennon, the City Council passed a resolution at the recommendation of then Councilman and current Parks Commissioner Henry Stern dedicating this portion of Central Park to Lennon's memory and naming it Strawberry Fields after the Beatles song. When they lived in the nearby Dakota on 72nd Street and Central Park West, John and his wife, Yoko Ono Lennon, adopted this landscape as their own favorite oasis in the Park. A gift from Yoko Ono Lennon to the Central Park Conservancy provided funds to restore and endow this living memorial.

The path is a loop that brings you back to the medallion past one of the most beautiful landscapes in the Park. At the bottom of the hill, note the six white pines—the largest of this species in the Park—that mark the end of the original Winter Drive. After completing the loop, walk out onto the Upper Meadow, an undulating lawn popular with picnickers. At the northernmost point of the meadow are three bald cypresses.

The slope behind the memorial is called Rose Hill for the rambling roses in the clefts of the bedrock. The eastern slope is a woodland popular with bird watchers. In its center is the Woodland Wildflower Meadow filled with ostrich and Christmas ferns and Virginia bluebells. In all, over 161 new plant species were introduced here, representing the various countries belonging to the United Nations.

An Oasis with a View
SUMMIT ROCK

West Side between 81st and 85th Streets

Summit Rock is the highest natural elevation in Central Park. Like Vista Rock, the site of Belvedere Castle, it is a massive bedrock outcrop. Summit Rock originally commanded a view across the Hudson River to the New Jersey Palisades, making it a logical place for Olmsted and Vaux to provide both a carriage and pedestrian overlook. Although the view has been reduced over the past 100 years to a sliver along West 83rd Street, it's still worthwhile to pause and relax on one of the stone benches on the Summit.

As in many parts of the Park, past landscape restorations had enjoyed brief popularity but had deteriorated with lack of maintenance. A recent restoration of Summit Rock now recaptures the spirit of the site and offers updated opportunities for its enjoyment. The broken 1950s pavement crowning Summit Rock was removed and a new green lawn added. There is a rustic stone "amphitheater"

with benches overlooking the wooded slopes to the south and east. Snaking up the southern slope is a serpentine path, recently recovered, with steps that were carved into the bedrock when the Park was built. Teachers can bring classes to the site for alfresco lessons on Park and City history, or even an impromptu dramatic performance. Practitioners of tai chi also enjoy the meditative quiet of the site.

Also on the southern slope is Tanner's Spring, named after a 19th century health practitioner who believed, it is said, that by drinking the spring's water he was able to stay healthy during a cholera epidemic that spread through New York State. The spring, too, had disappeared through neglect but now bubbles into shallow pools designed for bird bathing.

Before the City purchased the land and Central Park went into construction, the Summit Rock site, and others contiguous to it, were inhabited by some 5,000 New Yorkers, many of them new immigrants who could not afford the more expensive rents downtown. Roy Rosenzweig and Elizabeth Blackmar write in *The Park and the People* that more than 1,000 buildings dotted the landscape, most of them small dwellings but also taverns, barns, factories, and churches. In the 1830s Seneca Village, one of the City's best-known African American communities, was established in the West 80s on land occupied today by Summit Rock and the Arthur Ross Pinetum. By the 1850s Seneca Village—which had three churches, a school, and its own burial grounds—was an integrated community of almost 60 households. Most of the dwellings were inhabited by free black families, more than half of whom owned their own property.

Strings Attached

SWEDISH COTTAGE
MARIONETTE THEATER

**West Side at 79th Street
Summer and School Year Seasons
Suggested donation: Children $4; Adults $5
Further Information: 212-988-9093**

For over fifty years, puppeteers have been bringing to life magical tales of princesses, paupers, genies, and giants to hundreds of youngsters and their parents at Central Park's Swedish Cottage Marionette Theater. The company was founded in 1939 as a touring marionette theater and made the Swedish Cottage their headquarters after WWII. They are one of a few public marionette theater companies left in the U.S.—they write (or adapt) their own scripts, construct and costume the puppets, and design and produce every show themselves. Some of their favorites have been: *Cinderella, Jack and the Beanstalk,* and *Hansel and Gretel.*

The cottage was originally a schoolhouse sponsored by the Swedish government for the 1876 Centennial Exposition in Philadelphia as an example of Swedish building design. At the end of the exposition, the New York City Parks Department purchased the schoolhouse for $1,500 and moved it to its present site. Its first use was as a tool house; soon thereafter it was converted to a comfort station and lunchroom. After Swedish-Americans in the City complained about its inappropriate use, it was remodeled as the Park's entomological laboratory. In 1947 the building was retrofitted to house a small children's theater and design workshops. Today it is the headquarters for Citywide Puppets in the Parks program which is supported by the not-for-profit City Parks Foundation.

Recently the building has undergone a complete interior and exterior restoration. Today's visitors can enjoy the whimsical Scandinavian details inside the theater, along with seating for 100 children, central air conditioning, and a larger, state-of-the-art stage for more sophisticated productions. The original Baltic fir exterior was completely refurbished and details such as the second floor balcony were reconstructed. If there is any doubt that you have found the cottage, just look for the American and Swedish flags flying from its roof.

From Sheepfold to Crystal Palace

TAVERN ON THE GREEN

West Side between 66th and 67th Streets
Lunch: Weekdays noon to 3 pm and
weekends from 11 am
Dinner: Sunday—Thursday 5:30 pm—10:30 pm,
Friday and Saturdays 5 pm—11:45 pm;
Saturday and Sunday brunch: 10 am—3 pm
Pre-theater dinner: Monday—Friday, 5-6:30 pm
Reservations: 212-873-3200
Gift Shop • Valet Parking

With a half million patrons a year Tavern on the Green must be doing something right. Once home to Central Park's flock of sheep and its shepherd (see Sheep Meadow, page 118) the building was converted in the 1930s into a restaurant. But it wasn't until 1976, when Warner LeRoy became the proprietor, that the restaurant earned its current popularity.

To a degree unusual for a restaurant, the building itself is part of the dining experience. LeRoy spent over $10 million to refurbish the old Tavern. Crystal and mirrors and stained glass reflect light onto elaborate murals and works of art. There are six dining rooms reached through a twisting hall of mirrors. Three of the dining rooms—Crystal, Chestnut, and Park—form a horseshoe around a central garden. The largest, the Crystal Room, is filled with chandeliers—not to imply that other rooms do not have chandeliers as well; it's merely a matter of volume. The Chestnut Room is cozier, with chestnut-paneled walls and live entertainment. And the Park Room is smallest of all, overlooking the Tavern's main entrance with a park garden and a working fountain. Opposite the Chestnut Room is the Rafters Room with a high beamed ceiling; it too over-

looks the garden. A Crystal Gazebo room rounds out the end of the Crystal Room. And the Terrace Room overlooks Central Park West, with its own terrace garden.

In the garden outside the Crystal Room—weather permitting—you can enjoy a drink at the forty-foot bar built from pruned trees recycled from New York City parks. Seated at a table you can trade menacing gestures with a life-sized topiary gorilla or appreciate a prancing topiary horse frozen in time. In the garden visitors can see the original Victorian brick structure designed by Calvert Vaux. Minton tiles (see Bethesda Terrace, page 23) are used as a decorative element.

Both locals and tourists alike frequent Tavern on the

Green for another reason: to dine. Two signature dishes are Harvest Wild Mushroom Soup and Duck Crumble. The soup is flavored with truffle oil and porcini mushrooms. The duck is crispy, wrapped in a pastry shell, and served with sweet and sour onions and cilantro.

You can't miss this restaurant. Tiny white and blue lights outline every twig, branch, and trunk of its surrounding trees—a city substitute for stars in the night.

Love Means Keeping Score

TENNIS CENTER

Mid-Park between 94th and 96th Streets
April—November 6:30 am—dusk,
weather permitting
Seasonal Tennis Permit: Adults $50;
Seniors $20; Juniors $10
Public Restrooms, Pro shop, and Snack Bar
Permit Office: 212-280-0201

I f you are a tennis player or would like to become one, the purchase of a City Parks Department seasonal tennis permit is one of the best bargains in New York. With it you can play on any public tennis court in the City from April to November. City players consider Central Park's 26 Har-Tru and four-asphalt courts some of the best maintained in the City. In fact, in 1997 it won the Facility of the Year award from the U.S. Professional Tennis Registry.

To learn how to get you and your partner on the

courts, pick up information sheets when you buy your permit at the Central Park Arsenal. You also can purchase a single play ticket for $5 at the Tennis Center's snack bar. The Tennis Center also offers private lessons and sponsors clinics and tournaments.

The sport of tennis has been around in

various forms for a long time, but it wasn't until the 1870s that it began to take on mass popularity with the advent of lawn tennis in Britain. The craze quickly spread to the U.S. and was part of Central Park's gradual welcoming of sports activities. In the 1880s virtually all the open meadows in Central Park were limed out for temporary lawn tennis courts during the summer months. In the South Meadow tennis

became a permanent fixture first with asphalt courts and then with a large tennis house in 1930. The landscape between the Reservoir and the Tennis Center will undergo extensive restoration starting in 1999/2000.

Come Out of Your Shell
TURTLE POND

Mid-Park between 79th and 80th Streets

Seeing Turtle Pond for the first time—or any number of times—it's hard to believe that it was not part of the original Olmsted and Vaux design for Central Park. It seems perfectly suited to its location at the base of Belvedere Castle, and is a perfect watery complement to the Great Lawn. The visitor must remember, however, that the Great Lawn too was not original to the Park; it began life as the Croton Reservoir and was filled in with City building rubble in the 1930s (see page 63). The southern end was turned into Belvedere Lake, a shallow pond with a nondescript shape. Over the years Belvedere Lake developed a following: fish, frogs, turtles, dragonflies, and other aquatic creatures provided freely by nature. In 1987 it was renamed Turtle Pond in honor of its most conspicuous residents.

In 1997 Turtle Pond was part of the Great Lawn renovation, giving it an entirely new look. Landscape architects gave the shoreline a more irregular shape to maximize its length and follow more closely configurations of original Park lakes. They

added shoreline plants such as lizard's tail, bull rush, turtlehead, and blueflag iris which provide habitat for birds, insects, amphibians, and reptiles. All these plantings may look natural, but they rest on concrete shelves set at different depths under the surface of the pond that both support and contain the plants.

As part of the renovation, a new island—Turtle Island, not unexpectedly—was added to the pond. It serves as a wildlife habitat, providing sandy spots for turtles to lay their eggs and nesting and foraging sites for birds. A dock and a nature blind now extend into the pond, allowing visitors to see the dead tree trunks deliberately placed as sunning sites for turtles; frogs, herons, and other waterfowl are also claiming a perch. Fierce-looking dragonflies and damselflies have returned and are increasing in number; they are most active on the sunny north shore.

Visitors in the area on a Saturday afternoon may see the informal folk-dancing group that gathers under the statue of King Jagiello during the warmer months. The new plaza (with an image of a turtle in the bluestone pavement) was constructed to accommodate this traditional Polish and

Lithuanian activity and to provide an outdoor setting for nature studies. The equestrian statue by Stanislaw Kazimierz Ostrowski commemorates King Wladyslaw Jagiello, a Polish-Lithuanian hero of the

15th century. Jagiello was the first Christian Grand Duke of Lithuania who in 1410 led Polish and Lithuanian forces to victory over their long-time enemies, the Teutonic Knights of the Cross in the Battle of Grünwald.

Take to the Ice and Get in the Swim

WOLLMAN RINK

East Side between 62nd and 63rd Streets

LASKER RINK AND POOL

Mid-Park between 108th and 109th Streets

T he Wollman Rink was a success from the day it opened in 1949. Over 300,000 skaters glided across the ice in its first year of operation. Today over 4,000 use the Rink daily. Wollman's easy access from Grand Army Plaza (East 59th Street and Central Park South) and its picturesque location between the Dairy to the north and the Pond to the south make it popular not only for skaters, but also for any visitor who appreciates the romance of the New York City skyline. Spectators sitting on the outside bleachers—or skaters confident enough to look up—can see the skyscraper outline that makes a New York view distinct in the world.

Wollman hosts skaters day and night. But nighttime is a New York City moment. Music plays across the ice as skaters find their own rhythm circling the rink. A moon is a plus, but not required since the ice itself gives off a silver sheen. As the variety of accents testifies, New Yorkers and tourists alike mingle on the ice. The holiday season is undoubtedly the most popular—or at least the most picturesque. Children steal the scene: knit hats with pompoms, snowsuits inflated with useful padding, and standard issue red cheeks. If those cheeks get too red, skaters can go inside to an informal snack bar that serves assorted fast food, and hot and cold drinks.

Further north, at West 108th Street inside the Park, is Lasker Rink and Pool. Lasker was built in the 1960s and occupies a magnificent upper park site at the end of the Loch and overlooking the Harlem Meer (see Harlem Meer, page 65). Whereas Wollman converts its ice rink into a summertime miniature golf course and inline skating rink, Lasker's ice rink changes into a public swimming pool. In its ice skating mode, Lasker has two oval rinks: one for high school hockey teams and one for the public of all ages. The summer

swimming pool is obviously the most popular neighborhood retreat from New York's steaming summers. It's easy to find the pool even without a map, since the sounds of children in a pool in the summer are unmistakable.

Wollman Rink

Winter Ice Skating Oct. 15–March 31

- Open 7 days a week: Monday–Tuesday 10 am–3 pm, Wednesday–Thursday 10 am–5:30 pm, Friday–Saturday 10 am–11 pm, Sunday 10 am–9:30 pm
- Admission: $7 adults, $3.50 children and seniors
- Skate Rental: $3.50, Lockers available

Summer In-Line Skating May 1st–Labor Day

- Open Thursday–Sunday from 11 am–6 pm
- Admission: $4.00 adults, $3.00 children and seniors
- Skate Rental: $6.00
- Lessons available
- For information: 212-396-1010

Lasker Rink and Pool

Winter Ice Skating November–April

- Open Monday–Thursday from 10 am–3 pm; Friday from 10 am–2 pm and 5 pm–9 pm; Saturday from 11 am–10 pm; Sunday from 11 am–6 pm
- Admission: $3.00 adults, $1.50 children and seniors
- Skate Rental: $3.50

Summer Pool Opens July 1st and Closes after Labor Day

- Open 7 days a week from 11 am–7 pm
- Admission is free
- For information: 212-534-7639

Selected Bibliography

Barlow, Elizabeth, et al. *Rebuilding Central Park.* Cambridge, Massachusetts: The MIT Press, 1987.

Burnheim, Louise C. and George W. W. Packard. *Central Park: A Visit to One of the World's Most Treasured Landscapes,* New York, New York and Avenel, New Jersey: Crescent Books, 1993.

Burton, Dennis. *Nature Walks of Central Park.* New York, New York: Henry Holt and Company, Inc., 1997.

Gayle, Margot and Michele Cohen. *The Art Commission and the Municipal Art Society Guide to Manhattan's Outdoor Sculpture.* New York, New York: Prentice Hall Press, 1988.

Reed, Henry Hope and Sophia Duckworth. *Central Park: A History and a Guide.* New York, New York: Clarkson N. Potter, Inc., 1972.

Rosenzweig, Roy and Elizabeth Blackmar. *The Park and the People: A History of Central Park.* New York, New York: Henry Holt and Company, Inc., 1992.

CENTRAL PARK
59th Street to 85th Street

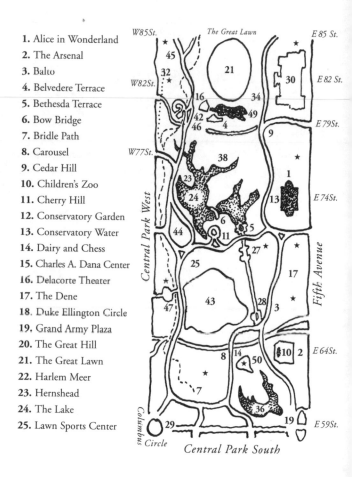

1. Alice in Wonderland
2. The Arsenal
3. Balto
4. Belvedere Terrace
5. Bethesda Terrace
6. Bow Bridge
7. Bridle Path
8. Carousel
9. Cedar Hill
10. Children's Zoo
11. Cherry Hill
12. Conservatory Garden
13. Conservatory Water
14. Dairy and Chess
15. Charles A. Dana Center
16. Delacorte Theater
17. The Dene
18. Duke Ellington Circle
19. Grand Army Plaza
20. The Great Hill
21. The Great Lawn
22. Harlem Meer
23. Hernshead
24. The Lake
25. Lawn Sports Center

LEGEND

Bridle Path ------------------
Playgrounds ★
Naturalists' Walk ••••••••••••••••

CENTRAL PARK
86th Street to 110th Street

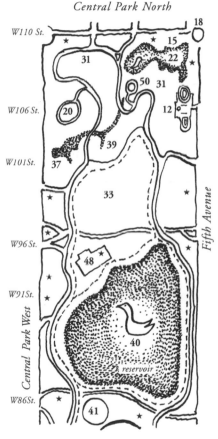

Central Park North

26. Loeb Boathouse
27. The Mall
28. Literary Walk
29. Merchants' Gate
30. Met. Mus. of Art
31. Military Fortifications
32. Naturalists' Walk
33. North Meadow
34. The Obelisk
35. Playgrounds
36. The Pond
37. The Pool
38. The Ramble
39. The Ravine
40. The Reservoir
41. Arthur Ross Pinetum
42. Shakespeare Garden
43. Sheep Meadow
44. Strawberry Fields
45. Summit Rock
46. Swedish Cottage
47. Tavern on the Green
48. Tennis Center
49. Turtle Pond
50. Wollman & Lasker

INDEX

Especially For CHILDREN

FOUNTAINS & MONUMENTS

GARDENS

INFORMATION CENTERS

POINTS OF INTEREST

RECREATION

RESTAURANTS & REFRESHMENTS

SCULPTURES

CENTRAL PARK CONSERVANCY

The Central Park Conservancy is a private, not-for-profit organization founded in 1980 that manages Central Park in partnership with the City of New York Parks & Recreation. Through private donations from individuals, foundations, and corporations, the Conservancy provides 80 percent of the Park's annual operating budget, funds major capital improvements, provides horticultural care and management, and offers programs for volunteers and visitors. The Conservancy invites all Central Park visitors to become partners in taking care of the Park to ensure that it remains a beautiful place for leisure, recreation, and the appreciation of nature.

Beginning July 1999 visit us on the web at
www.centralparknyc.org

About the Authors

Karen H. Putnam has been with the Central Park Conservancy since 1993, first as Vice President and then as President beginning in 1996. She graduated from Wellesley College and has a Ph.D. in American Studies from Yale University. She has worked at Harvard and Yale Universities, the University of Pennsylvania, the Open University in London, and The Brooklyn Museum. She is the recipient of research and teaching fellowships in the fields of American literature and the history of higher education. A major fan of New York City as well as of Central Park, she recently was named a partner in the New York City Partnership and Chamber of Commerce, Inc. She resides in Manhattan.

Marianne Cramer is an Associate Professor at the University of Georgia School of Environmental Design. During her fifteen-year tenure as the Central Park Planner and landscape architect, she co-authored *Rebuilding Central Park: A Management and Restoration Plan*, the blueprint for the current restoration; initiated the Conservancy's innovative woodlands restoration program; and introduced several generations of staff to the Olmstedian tradition. She grew up on a dairy farm about two-thirds the size of Central Park near Freeport, Pennsylvania and now resides in the midst of Spanish oaks and Southern magnolias in the classical city of Athens.

About the Artist

With his folding chair, sketchbook, and bottle of ink, **John Coburn** is happiest working on location. He exhibits in New York and Toronto, where he lives with his wife Leslie, and their two children. He is represented by Beckett Fine Art. John also did the drawings for *New York's 50 Best Wonderful Little Hotels*.